# The Female
# VETERAN

# The Female VETERAN

## Ty Will

*The Female Veteran*

Copyright © 2024 by Tammy Wonder-Trevino. All rights reserved.

No part of this publication may be reproduced, stored in a retrieval system or transmitted in any way by any means, electronic, mechanical, photocopy, recording or otherwise without the prior permission of the author except as provided by USA copyright law.

The opinions expressed by the author are not necessarily those of URLink Print and Media.

1603 Capitol Ave., Suite 310 Cheyenne, Wyoming USA 82001
1-888-980-6523 | admin@urlinkpublishing.com

URLink Print and Media is committed to excellence in the publishing industry.

Book design copyright © 2024 by URLink Print and Media. All rights reserved.

Published in the United States of America

Library of Congress Control Number: 2024910145
ISBN 978-1-68486-777-6 (Paperback)
ISBN 978-1-68486-779-0 (Digital)

07.05.24

# Forward

Why does one join the armed forces? Do they join for glory? Do they join for patriotism? Do they join for the GI Bill? Do they join for revenge? I can't answer why others have joined; I can only answer why I joined.

As a second grader coming home from school a kid got out his BB gun and started to shot, that's when I got shot in the cheek. When my mom showed up, she asked me for the BB that was twirling around in my mouth. After, I spit the BB into my mom's hand I thought WOW that was cool. Ever since that moment I had a fascination with the military.

As I grew up and became a teenager I soon became fascinated with the ROTC program and wanted to go into ROTC but that was for the geeks in school, so I never joined-I sure wanted too. I wished I would have joined because you get to be a PFC (private first class) as you entered into boot camp which meant platoon leader. Who's the geek now?

Life has a funny way of turning things around; I was married young the first time. I was 17 by 18 I had my son. The marriage didn't last. I was married again at age 19 and had my daughter at 20. Once again that marriage didn't last. I am not going to go into why those marriages didn't last because that's another book. As I was watching TV one day, I saw a commercial for the Army and that's the moment I decided to do something for myself and my children. My parents took custody of the children until after I got out. It was a chance to learn a skill and come home and take care of my children.

I joined the Army Reserves in 1987; I trained as an operating room technician. I signed up for active duty in 1989. At this time I switched from operating room tech. to satellite communications because there wasn't a position open for OR Tech.

By the time I got into active duty I remarried and was ready to get my kids and move forward however, my son was in school and instead of taking him out of school I left him with my parents, my daughter came with me.

I had high hopes and expectations for the Army, a chance to be a better parent and a better person. I really enjoyed boot camp and the two training courses I went through. I was being sent to my first duty station. I loved the other soldiers and the fact that our unit was different. We got to travel to different locations around the world to set up communications.

I expected a since of honor, and a since of adventure with my first mission. What I got was not what I expected or would wish on any young female soldier.

3,000 female veterans file MST (military sexual trauma) reports every year, an unknown survey was sent out to all military branches and estimated 19,000 came back saying they were sexual harassed by someone in the direct chain of command, that's more than 50 female veterans a day. Reported by SAPRO.

## I AM ONE OF THESE WOMEN

My only hope is that the care for our female veteran's changes and that filing a case for MST goes straight to JAG and not into the direct chain of command, then and only then will there be a difference made.

This book is dedicated to all the female veterans too afraid to come out of the shadows.

*Chapter*

# 1

The following is a diary of my Mental Health Notes from 2001-2010. The real names have been changed.

**Progress Notes**                        **November 3, 2001**

35 year old female veteran referred by Dr. Cruz who saw her in employee health primary care clinic, female veteran works as telephone operator here at VA.

Patent was seen in crisis intervention. She mostly talked about getting stressed out over her relationship with husband whom she describes as controlling, suspicious, and mean to kids.

Tearful, depressed, no suicidal thoughts, anxious but towards the end of session with crisis intervention was feeling quite positive, relieved and reassured, smiled and no suicide hallucination's ideations were verbalized.

Adjustment disorder with depressed mood.

Will increase zooloft to 100 mg a day and temporarily add temazepam for insominia.

/es/ Neil Neiz M.D.

Author Notes: I started to work at the VA as a telephone operator and realized while working at the VA that any veteran can get help at the VA. I always thought you had to be a combat Veteran to get help.

I don't know how I feel about mental health. I thought that you sat on a couch and talk, like in the movies. However, it was just a cold metal chair telling the doctor how overwhelmed I felt. Welcome to the VA mental health system.

**Progress Notes**                                    **November 9, 2001**

Female veteran here for follow up, No change in complaining style. No new substance into her complaints which almost sounds like whining.

Nothing she wants to do about it, wants to wait until some money is saved up so she can finally move out.

Slept very well with restoril. Will not renew restoril.

/es/ Neil Neiz M.D.

Author Note: When I get upset my voice changes, this Dr. Neiz makes me angry for she talks about how I sound like I'm whining. I thought going to therapy was to talk about your problems not get criticized by the therapist for the way your voice sounds when it gets upset. Fuck you doctor Neiz!!!!

**Progress Notes**                                    **February 26, 2002**

Female veteran here after some absence from therapy and stated things have changed a lot. Husband was hurt in near death accident; realization is from both sides about what "we have", and therefore atmosphere at home is much better. Veteran stated she feel quite stable at current doses of meds, not so upset, able to handle crisis much better.

Renew meds unchanged.

/es/ Neil Neiz M.D.

Author Notes: My husband, at this time, was hit by a car and had to be life flight up to Billings for internal bleeding. This accident changed everything about what I was feeling before and how I was handling my emotions now. I felt closer to my husband, felt like he really needed me and that I was important to him.

## Progress Notes                              February 28, 2002

Time spent with female veteran 15 min

Returns for follow up; she was scheduled with Dr. Neilson but he was running behind and she had to get to a part time job so, I saw her briefly. Female veteran reports she was sexually harassed while on active duty and that she has never been the same. She is jumpy, has recurring nightmares, is distant from her husband and has no interest in sex. She is depressed but is better on the sertraline. The vet says she stays at home most of the time, is tired much of the time. She tried stopping the sertraline, became more depressed and has been back on meds for a month. She saw DR. Strong in town and talks to him about what she suffered in the military and he told her she suffers from PTSD, which I agree.

timid, shy, somewhat overweight, fearful, intermittent eye contact, affect restricted, mood depressed, rational; has constant anxiety; no delusion or hullications but problems with flashbacks, panic social avoidance and typical history of PTSD. Sensroium is not clouded but her attention is down.

PTSD, chronic, non-combat secondary to sexual trauma while on active duty; associated depression

Continue sertraline 100mg qd, return in 2-3 weeks with me or Dr. Neilson

/es/ Daniel Swartz M.D.

Author Notes: I was struggling, with not only emotions from my husband's accident but, from the stress of the situation. The accident had brought back the nightmares from what happened to me in the Army and I knew I needed help.

## Progress Notes                                                August 9, 2002

08/09/2002 addendum

Patient reassigned to Dr. Swartz per Dr. Swartz

Dr. Swartz has requested female veteran see social therapist for therapy

Status completed 08/09/2002

Author Notes: He requested that I see a therapist that specialized in MST (Military Sexual Trauma). I really thought that would be my chance to get some real help. Little did I know what would be involved in getting "Real Help".

## Progress Notes                                                October 10, 2002

MST Counseling Consult Report

Met with female veteran x90min as a result from consult.

She reported coming to this apt because the Dr. encouraged her to consider that the stress and depression in her life could be related to sexual trauma experienced. She blurted out that she would be happy for the rest of her life if she didn't have sex again.

After some inquiry of her history, she laughed into extensive disclosure about her multiple marriages, weeping at memories that surfaced, verbally resisting further discloser, and mentioned in passing that of "maybe" being sexually harassed in the military. She finally concluded that the origin of her sexual trauma was not from the military.

She describes personal losses, evidence awareness much emotional turmoil since being abused in her first relationship. Female veteran agrees to come back for further sessions.

Depression resulting from trauma

Return for another apt.

Janet Drapper

L.C.S.W.

Author Note: I was not comfortable talking about what happened. I didn't want to come forward and did not elaborate because I did not want to talk about that experience with someone I didn't know and didn't trust. I had just met this doctor and felt uncomfortable with her.

Notes from the above therapist caused the appeals that I made for the MST case to be dismissed. I didn't trust the Dr. and didn't want to talk about the rape. So I lied to the Dr. because, I didn't want to be labeled a nutcracker/mental case.

## Progress Notes                         November 22, 2002

Time spent with female veteran 30 min

Female veteran was seen for follow up today; I had seen her once before briefly and obtained more history today; she reports that she has had an aversion to sex since she was harassed in the military. She has some conflict with her husband and blames herself for this. She has difficulty falling asleep and fragmented sleep and tends to doze off during the day. She continues to be depressed but is tolerating the meds fine (except constipation); she spends her day doing household chores, working on the internet and watching TV. Husband works fulltime. She has 2 children from previous marriages at home 16yr old daughter and 10 year old son. She has been married 5 times, history of heavy alcohol use in the past but not for past year. Very self-deprecating, no suicide ideation at this time

spontaneous, well groomed, eye contact; some tearfulness; restricted affect; depressed mood; no suicide ideation; rational, no delusion or hallucination; very anxious and some history of panic, nightmares, chronic chest pain being evaluated by primary care. Sensorium not clouded

PTSD, chronic

Personality disorder

add quetiapine 25-50mg qhs continue sertraline

Emphasized need for continued follow up for psychotherapy

Daniel Swartz MD

Authors Note; I don't mind coming to this Dr. He seems to care for what happens to the veterans. I am really struggling with these panic attacks.

Personality disorder??? Really, at least I have one. WTF! I looked up personality disorder and there are 4. Everyone I know fits one of these categories. Who came up with this shit? I like my personality and if you don't like it- piss off.

**Progress Notes**                              **January 02, 2003**

Time spent with female veteran; 20 min.

Returns for follow up, stopped the wellbutrin as it was constipating; female veteran has not follow up with Janet Drapper for therapy and is encouraged to do Vet describes frequent panic attacks and a frequent recurring nightmare in which she wakes up in panic and is unable to speak. She is doing some aerobic exercises and plans to attend College to study radiology tech. She is working at her relationship with her husband. We discussed her moods which do change with circumstances but she denies suicide at this time.

sad appearing women, mood depressed and anxious with history of panic attacks PTSD, chronic noncombat

will give veteran trail of gabapentin which may help with neuropathic pain and benefit to stabilizing her moods, continue the sertiline and make follow up apt with Janet Drapper for therapy; return to see me in one month.

/es/ Daniel Swartz MD

Author Notes: I have had two recurring nightmares since leaving the Army. One I feel is evil and the other creates panic. In the evil nightmare I am frozen in my body and a black mass starts to invade my head and flows out of my toes. I can't scream- I can't move. In the panic dream I am being chased by a tornado.

I was just given medicine and therapy this is what is done at the VA.

At this point I didn't have a therapist at least one that I trusted. I didn't follow up with Dr. Drapper as I did not feel comfortable with her. I think one of the reasons for not trusting her is her constant reference to baby steps-what the fuck? Do I look like a child? Don't answer that!

## Progress Notes                    January 15, 2003

Time spent with female veteran x 60 min.

Last time she had been seen by this MST (Military Sexual Trauma) counselor was in Oct.

Today, she was angry, tearful, resentful, distrustful, and entwined emotions and events over the holidays, describing some emotionally charged situations and negative responses.

She had made genuine attempts of not putting herself down with a focused direction she was able to see herself at a different place less depressed than she had been over the holidays. This awareness she apparently did not have when she walked in today.

She reported by the end of this session that she "really wanted to change", even though she dreaded having to talk about it, and resistant to doing so.

PTSD; depression

Schedule with MST counselor next appointments

/es/ Janet Drapper

L.C.S.W.

Author Note: I was still uncomfortable with social worker. It may not have been the social worker so much as what they wanted me to talk about. To be honest my family **NEVER** talks about their feelings ever! Growing up we didn't see any emotions in the family. We didn't say I love you or kiss or really hug each other. It was always about what needed to be done and not about how we feel. Avoidance is my best defense against having to talk about the rape. If I avoid the topic it didn't happen in my mind.

## Progress Notes     May 21, 2003

Met with female veteran x 50min

Veteran begins today by talking about an event this past weekend that she is upset about. She says she wanted to go out for her birthday and do some drinking but her husband doesn't like for her to drink so she got drunk. There is also an issue about not having sexual relations as often as her husband wants. Explored briefly with female veteran her understanding of the origin of her aversion to sex and affection in general, She becomes more upset and expresses that she feels angry with her husband that he will not "just accept me the way I am." I talked with her about the origins of anger in general and emotional maturity.

Will return next week for MH (mental Health) intake and treatment planning.

/es/ Kristi Olsen

MSW

Author Note: Another new therapist, at least she doesn't say baby steps all the time. Ugh if I hear that saying one more time- I'll take a baby step outta here.

I saw nothing wrong with going out for a few drinks on my birthday.

At this point in my life I was a stay at home mom. I wanted to go out and have fun. I wanted do something besides stay at home all day. Boring!!!! Don't get me wrong I love my kids but sometimes a girl has to let loose and why not your birthday?

**Progress Notes**　　　　　　　　　　　　　　May 27, 2003

Met with female veteran x 50min

Completed MH (mental Health) intake, Female veteran and her family will be going on family vacation next week. Husband got settlement from near death accident he was in. She wants to begin therapy when she returns. She is cooperative with interview.

/es/ Kristi Olsen

MSW

**Progress Notes**　　　　　　　　　　　　　　June 23, 2003

Met with female veteran x 50 min

Veteran talks about her recent family vacation and how much fun they had. She reports feeling better. Mood is better and she says she is more tolerant of others and has been doing more which she attributes to an increase in antidepressant medication. She is reluctant to talk about PTSD issues especially as they relate to her marital relationship, suggested that she get a copy of "Courage to Heal" and read the sections that most apply to her. She agrees to do this. "You know I hate coming up here, don't you?" Need to continue to build rapport with female veteran.

/es/ Kristi Olsen

MSW

Author note: I did not get the book "Courage to Heal" I do not like to sit down and read.

This vacation was amazing!

Vacation was also hard because there were six kids and the age range was from 16 to 9. They all wanted to experience different things all at the same time. This vacation was extremely overwhelming to do everything all at once to please everyone but, I have to tell you it was one hell of a vacation. We went to Las Vegas to Excalibur, California to Disney Land, and Universal. Disney Land really is the happiest place on earth!!!

# Chapter 2

**Progress Notes**                                June 27, 2003

Mental Status:

Appearance: neatly groomed

Behavior Attitude: cooperative

Affect and Mood: agitated

Speech: normal

Thought content and process: normal

Suicidal/Homicidal Ideation: denies

Orientation: x3

Memory: intact

Fund of knowledge: good

Insight: limited

Strengths and weaknesses: Female veteran Identifies her strengths as "good cook, good mom, good personality, sense of humor" Weaknesses identified "I don't know, low self-esteem I guess"

## INTEGRATED BIOPSYCHOSOCIAL SUMMARY

Female veteran is a 37 year old seeking treatment for marital problems, depressed mood and symptoms of PTSD. PTSD symptoms are a result of sexual assault while on active duty ARMY.

She is the mother of 3 children ages are 18, 16, 10 who have different fathers. She is in her 5th marriage. Female veteran was in the Army from 1987-1992 and then in the reserves until 1995. She liked her duties as an operating room specialist while in the Army. Currently she is taking courses in College with the idea of becoming a radiology tech.

Alcohol has been a problem for veteran in the past. She says she quit drinking 5 years ago but talked about getting drunk on her last birthday. She is not interested in seeking treatment at this time.

No legal issues pending.

Diminished social functioning, Female veteran says she doesn't like to leave her house however, this seem to be getting less difficult since starting meds.

Diagnosis:

AXIS I: PTSD; Depression

AXIS II; Deferred

AXIS III;

AXIS IV; marital problems

AXIS V; GAF 62

Plan and Recommendation

Continued medication management with DR. Swartz; individual psychotherapy for PTSD and marital problems.

/es/ Kristi Olsen MSW

Authors note: I liked this therapist; I was more willing to open up to her. I had 2 MOS (Jobs) in the Army the 1st was 91delta Operating Room Specialist and 31 Quebec Satellite Communications. The rape occurred while I was doing my 2nd enlistment as a 31Q.

I did have a drinking problem, after getting out of the military, which lasted several years.

I don't know why they keep bringing up how many times I was married, ugh!

## Progress Notes                            June 28, 2003

Met with female veteran x 20 min

Much improved with combination of psychotherapy and Effexor. Veteran tolerated lower dose of this. Only side effect is some constipation. Not as irritable, able to enjoy life and getting along better with her husband. Sleep has improved as well. She just got back from a trip that included Las Vegas, Disneyland and San Diego. She is now filing a claim for MST as I have encouraged her to do.

Pleasant, friendly, less anxious, some eye contact, affect brighter; no Del or hall; sensorium clear

PTSD, chronic (noncombat)

Continue Effexor. I have encouraged her to continue psychotherapy with Kristi Olsen. Return in 3 months

/es/ David P. Schultz MD

Author note: Dr. advised to file a MST case. Thought this would give me closure. However, filing this case was one of the hardest things I have ever done. I had to write the event down on paper and it was reliving the rape all over again.

The Cheyenne VA made this difficult; everything was looked at under a microscope. They made me feel as though this incident was my fault and that I was on trial. Looking back I truly wish I hadn't of filed for compensation.

## Progress Notes                                    July 9, 2003

Met with female veteran x75 min

Veteran begins today by talking about her most recent nightmare which caused her not to want to sleep for 2 days, she says she got some sleep and is feeling better now. I encouraged her to talk about her dream as she refers to as being "evil".

She is more candid today and is open to the idea of resolving her past so that she can be a better mother and partner. I reviewed with her the informational video on EMDR(Eye Movement Desensitization Reprocessing). She is interested in the technique and wants to try EMDR next week.

/es/ Kristi Olsen

MSW

Author Note: I'm looking forward to and scared to try EMDR. I'm scared to remember what happen but also wanting to move forward.

I'm scared because I'm comfortable living in this deep end of the pool called depression. It's my survival mode. To do something new means treading out of the comfortable warm spot in the pool of depression. I'm not sure I can do it or willing to even try but try I must because this is no way of living life.

## Progress Notes                                         August 14, 2003

Time spent with female veteran x20 min

Vet is doing well on the effort at low dose; mood overall improved but she has had some conflicts within her family. She and her husband are split up due to increase abuse. Vet is seeing social worker for counseling here and has filed claim for MST.

Pleasant, friendly spontaneous women, affect bright and appropriate, has some vivid dreams now, sensorium is clear.

PTSD, chronic (non-combat)

Continue venlafaxine return 2-3 months

/es/ Daniel Swartz MD

Author Note: YAYYYYYYYYY!!!! Spilt up with dick weed couldn't wait to get divorced from him. My children and I no longer have to face abuse from him. Incident that put me over the top was when he physically abused my daughter. Dickweed made her sit at the kitchen table and wouldn't let her leave. When my daughter got up to leave dickweed grab her around the waist and accidently rip her skin, where she was sunburn. One week after I moved out, he moved his girlfriend in. Like I said he's a dickweed!

**Progress Notes**                                                   **August 27, 2003**

Met with female veteran x 50 min

Female veteran says that she will be moving to an apartment this week and her divorce will be final in Sept. She hopes that she and her husband will continue to work on their relationship even after the divorce.

MST issue rose as a factor in the decline of the marriage. Veteran is very reluctant to address the MST issue. She has started the paper work to file a claim for PTSD related to the MST. She is finding that to be very difficult and she questions whether she wants to continue with the claim. She is tearful at times. Did a relaxation technique before she left the office which she said was very helpful.

/es/ Kristi Olsen

MSW

Author Note: Family pressure to make things work but I knew in my heart that I would not be able to do so. I really did not want to go back to dickweed and I was happy being by myself no fear of being locked in the bathroom until I agreed with him, no fear of my kids being hit, him hiding the food. Ugh! glad to be free!

**Progress Notes**                                          **November 17, 2003**

Female veteran seen in walk in clinic today

Veteran says she has been having trouble sleeping because of her stress around her impending divorce. She is often tearful and is tired. She recently began work at the Veterans Home of Wyoming. Today she wants to vent some of her frustration and anger about her situation, which she does. She denies suicidal ideation. She agrees to no self-harm contract. She will schedule an appointment for further support.

/es/ Kristi Olsen

MSW

Author note: The stress of the divorce brought out a lot of anger issues and I started having nightmares more than three times a week. I kept getting harassed by the head housekeeper at work which brought on more stress and heightened the PTSD symptoms.

Wow! Head housekeeper there's a job you want when you grow up- really? She had nothing better to do then spy on me?? She counted all the soaps in my closet to make sure I was using them in the rooms and the only reason I know this is I found the paper with this info on it. Crazy Bitch

## Progress Notes                        December 18, 2003

Time spent with female veteran x 20 min

37 yr old female veteran reports persistent insomnia, nocturnal panic which is relieved by low dose lorazepam. Tearful off and on during the session; some depression and loss of weight noted since divorce went through. No active suicide ideation. Female veteran working at vets home and enjoys that; this is her 5th divorce and she feels a failure at marriage. Not much social life now with 3 kids at home.

Primary Diagnosis; history consistent with PTSD, non-combat

/es/ Daniel Swartz MD

Author Note: I guess everyone losses weight after a divorce. Stressed would be an understatement considering I went from an income of 5000 a month to 1000.

I did like working at the vets home, enjoyed working with the veterans and I even let them get away with things that Attila the Hun would not let them get away with- like walking down the hallway with an open container. Hell I let them carry open food down the hallways just hoping they would drop something just so, I could hear her get mad. bahahaha

## Progress Notes                                  February 13, 2004

Met with female veteran x 50 min

Female veteran upset today about her claim being denied, she states "the compensation department said that because she stated in one of her first apt. up here that ""maybe"" something might of happened that it didn't happen, they (compensation) said because she was married so many times was the reason for the PTSD not MST so claim was denied, she is very angry about being thrown under the bus."

Female veteran was able to calm herself. She is able to verbalize an understanding that she needs to resolve with the past. She reports fewer nightmares and has less frequent intrusive recollections of military sexual trauma, she then goes on to say her divorce is finale from" dickweed", she is employed at vets home and has recently purchased a mobile home. Her eldest son has come to live with her. He found a job and she says is a big help. She has some medical issues that may require surgery so she is grateful for his help. She talks at length about her relationship with her children has improved. "We laugh all the time and have fun now"

Mood appears to have improved, affect is bright.

/es/ Kristi Olsen

MSW

Author Note: Cheyenne VA denied case and instead of looking at the evidence only looked at the one report. They also told me the reason I got out of the Army was I got pregnant by another man not my husband-true this is -but if the Army would have let me out on hardship I would not of gotten pregnant to get out-I saw no option for me at the time.

The VA always denies MST cases; military does not want to face this issue. Instead of looking at all the indicators in my military file they only looked at what they wanted to see and used that against me. Did what they could so they wouldn't have to feel responsible. Rape is treated different then combat PTSD. As if I'm a second class solider that doesn't deserve the time or respect.

I don't understand why they have to keep bringing up my marriages it's a constant slap in the face with how much of a failure I am. Don't they realize it wasn't the marriages but the trauma?

## Progress Notes                                April 01, 2004

Met with female veteran x 20 min

Female veteran is seeing Social Worker for psychotherapy and takes a low dose Effexor for depression; says she is anxious and has panic attacks almost daily; works at vets home but has been having problems with her supervisor and filed a grievance for harassment which may be the cause of her panic attacks co – related to harassment from military.

Female veteran was turned down for her claim for PTSD and is appealing which I have encouraged. I discussed her meds with her and her relationship for continuing therapy. Female veteran may be starting EMDR soon.

Anxious, tearful off and on, affect mildly labile, mood depressed. Tapping foot constantly and minimal eye contact, rational and logical; no Del or hall present

/es/ Daniel Swartz MD

Author Note: Cheyenne VA denied PTSD claim. They are notorious for turning down claims that are in conjunction with MST. Once again I felt let down and that I wasn't validated even though the incident was in my record. Once again I feel like a second class solider not worthy of respect because the issue is rape.

Work seemed almost unbelievable that someone thinks they can harass you without repercussions. Yes, I did file a claim against my boss; you can't treat people in lower positions in the manner which she treated me. Even-though, we were only in housekeeping she felt like she was Queen Bee of the Vets Home.

I was not the only one who had problems with her, but I was the only one not afraid to stand up for myself.

The head housekeeper did get reprimanded for harassing me, she got 60 days of DO NOT TALK to me, and a grievance in her personnel file. I was happy with the outcome, after this I moved into working in the kitchen

# Chapter 3

**Progress Notes**　　　　　　　　　　　**April 2, 2004**

Met with female veteran x 50 min

Veteran is upset today and angry that a man she was in a relationship with had been cheating on her. We discussed relationship issues and I encouraged her to refrain from romantic relationships for a few months until she is feeling more stable and secure. This lead to a discussion of using EMDR to resolve past trauma issues, she says she is afraid the EMDR will make her remember things she does not want to remember. Asked her to seriously consider EMDR and that it is impossible to know what she will experience in the course of treatment but that experience tells me that issues that need to be resolved will surface and they can be addressed rather quickly through the use of EMDR, Also told her that she will not need to go into details of any memory unless she chooses to do so.

/es/ Kristi Olsen

MSW

Author Note: I really hate the fact that I got into another relationship in which a guy cheated on me you would think I would learn a lesson but I don't. Can you really give up on love? I mean there has to be someone out there that will cherish the love you give freely, hopefully, for why else are we here if not to learn how to love and give love?

EMDR is a form of therapy that uses rapid hand movement and I was scared that my brain had forgotten these things for a reason. I didn't want to get those memories back. I wanted to protect myself from more pain. Yup, avoidance my main issue.

## Progress Notes          May 18, 2004

Met with female veteran x 30 min

Veteran comes in today very upset over "dickweeds" accusations of stalking charges filed against her. She denies any such activities; she will go to court this afternoon. Allowed her to vent and she felt better. She will reschedule apt. for EMDR.

Diagnosed; PTSD, non-combat

/es/ Kristi Olsen

MSW

Author Note: First of all, I did not stalk him!!!! Was accused of stalking him, he really just wanted to cause more problems for me. In the divorce, I got the better deal.

In court this case was dismissed because he had no evidence to back his claims. He's a dickweed!

## Progress Notes          June 03, 2004

Met with female veteran x 20 min

Veteran very tearful, angry, anxious, defensive, says she wants to go to sleep and is tired, ran out of her meds, Says she is involved in new relationship and this is stressful to her, still problems with ex(court case was dismissed lack of evidence) . Goes to bar a lot gets drunk, got into a fight with another women at bar last night was some pushing and shoving, vet is seeing Kristi Olsen and has another apt; vet denies active suicidal ideation but does get hopeless feeling, I discussed hosp. but she denies adamantly against that.

Objective, tearful, no active suicide ideation, rational and logical, has panic attacks and panic dreams

Primary diagnosis: PTSD, chronic, non-combat,

/es/ Daniel Swartz MD

Author Note: So at this point I was dating this guy I worked with. Some of us are very slow learners, it is important to not dip your quill in the company ink. Wink, Wink, awkward as all get out, advice to all: don't date someone you work with!

My son had come back to live with us and got his GED. My daughter was a junior in high school. My other son was in middle school.

Yes, still drinking, you would too if you had my life.

## Progress Notes                                      July 17, 2004

Met with female veteran x 60 min

She reports that the "evil" nightmare continues to haunt her although not as frequent as in the past. She recognizes that when she is feeling stress the nightmares return. Female veteran is more open today about discussing MST issues. Allowed her to talk about her impressions of her MST and the anger she feels toward the attacker. She expresses self-blame for the incident" I shouldn't have opened the door"

The relationship with her mother is conflicted and confusing for her. "Sometimes she is nice then other times not so nice."

Brought up the EMDR again, she is afraid to bring it up all again, suggest it might help with her "evil" nightmare. She will consider it.

Veteran has admitted to drinking excessively 1-2 times per week, she sees no harm in this.

/es/ Kristi Olsen

MSW

Author Note: The evil nightmare haunts me; however the less stress that I have the less I have this dream. I want to resolve the MST issue by doing the EMDR. I am hoping this will help in moving forward-past the trauma.

Yes, I liked alcohol, it made me numb. Gees' get off my back for drinking, there's worse things I could have been doing.

# Chapter

# 4

**Progress Notes**  October 14, 2004

Met with female veteran x 50 min

Veteran is upset today she feels the VA is not listening to her, she feels that there is something wrong with her yet she doesn't know what it is, "the Va thinks it's all in my head but it's not, I'm so tired all the time, I'm tired of being tired and I have some kind of twitching in my muscles that have just popped up out of no-where. I would like to curl up in bed and sleep for a couple of weeks." After venting anger and frustration with the VA, she was more willing to look at issues that relate to MST. She continues to focus on the "why's" why did I open the door? Why did I go into the Army? I talked with veteran about letting go of the past and working on self-forgiveness. Vet says" I have to get on with my life"

Recommend that she write a letter of forgiveness.

/es/ Kristi Olsen

MSW

Author note: I never wrote that freakin letter of forgiveness. Why the hell would I write that? I don't feel like I need to forgive myself or him in particular. I now know why I opened that door, because he was my SGT and I had to obey orders. What some people, that haven't been in the military, don't understand is that you have to obey orders otherwise, you get an article 15. An article 15 is basically a bad mark in your record. Nobody listen to me in the ARMY when I told them the Sargent was harassing me- absolutely no-one.

## Progress Notes                                October 14, 2004

Met with female veteran x 20 min

Veteran says she is not sleeping any better and is tired all the time; she is working and attending some college classes and has family but that she is only sleeping about 2-3 hours per night. Discussed with her the chronic insomnia and she does have nightmares associated with being assaulted in the past she is reluctant to talk about it. Veteran Admits to drinking at times.

Objective: tearful off and on; affect labile; mood with depression but no si present, rational and logical

PTSD chronic, non-combat

/es/ Daniel Swartz MD

Author Note: Sleep deprivation does not help with the stress. My moods at this time were a little all over the place. I felt like the VA wasn't doing enough. I felt like no-one was listening to me. My chest started to hurt, it would freeze up. I thought I was going to die of a heart attack. The reality of the chest pains was just panic attacks from too much stress and drinking only made it worse.

## Progress Notes                                February 03, 2005

Met with female veteran x55 min

Veteran spends most of the session talking about her physical condition and the stress she feels at work. She is off work this week for rest due to her increased fatigue. Veteran eventually gets around to talking about her anger toward her family. Also talked about her level of stress and how she is able to control it with some cognitive restricting. She asked about EMDR beginning to realize that she must get some resolution about the past before she can move on with her life.

Scheduled EMDR session to focus on sexual assault trauma

/es/ Kristi Olsen MSW

Author Note: I really needed to do something about the level of stress, so I conceded to doing the EMDR.

*Chapter*

# 5

**Progress Notes**                      **February 16, 2005**

Met with female veteran x 50 min

PSYCHIATRY NOTE

Chief complaint chest pains, was transferred her by primary care, chest pains not from cardiac nature.

Female veteran new to unit 8 and will be processed in.

She is working and told her boss that her chest was hurting and getting feedback that nothing is wrong with her except PTSD. She complains that her body hurts all over.

Past PSYCHIATRIC HISTORY:

Was treated in military (91-92) treated for suicidal thoughts in Germany-seen by local Psychiatrist several sessions.

Summary and Formulation: female veteran is an interesting patient. She carries a list of multiple medical concerns and MST related issues. She has had quite traumatic life story of 5 divorces, three children all from different men, and ultimately adding to the MST she was recently diagnosed with Lupus. She expresses her feelings of despair and frustration stating she has been undermined because everyone including her boss feels she is okay and nothing is wrong but her PTSD. Patient has valid reason to feel this way.

She has indeed many medical and psychiatric illnesses that seem to overlap and toward the end all need to be appropriately addressed for this patient to receive the most effective care possible.

Axis I PTSD, non-combat

Axis II Personality disorder with borderline

Axis III SLE Lupus

Plan: Patient is admitted to ward

/es/ Franco Dells

M.D. Psychiatrist

Author Note: First time being put in unit 8 lockdown having gotten overwhelmed with life. Really needed help to gain a better understanding of where I was presently and what I needed to do in order to have a better future. This really gave me the time to analyze and gain perspective. I was also able to relax and get some much needed sleep.

**Progress Notes**                                          **February 16, 2005**

Female Veteran seen with team today

She states she doesn't need to be here (unit 8). Female veteran state since she was diagnosed with Lupus she has had a hard time dealing with life and has given up. "What else can go wrong"? She is having intrusive thoughts that she didn't like, hospitalization was recommended by her primary care provider.

Related thoughts "thoughts about killing myself... I didn't feel my life was worth living anymore... but I wouldn't act on it" Veteran admits that a couple weeks ago of making a plan to cut her wrists.

Depressed for past month, she is not hearing voices. Female veteran states she won't act on her thoughts that she would talk to somebody if that changed. Female Veteran lives with her children, states feeling angry about past, present, not feeling as though being listened too. Female Veteran has been seen in social therapy. Afraid she will lose her job at vet's home, appeared tearful and anxious.

Plan- discussed with vet recommendation for continued treatment, she request to be released she doesn't feel she will act on suicide ideation, will release veteran.

## Progress Notes                    February 16, 2005

Female veteran seen1:1 discussed again with her the recommendations for continued treatment. Female Veteran continues to request discharge. Female Veteran states feeling selfish for coming, considering trying to split her work schedule so, she won't tire as easily. Veteran thinks about suicide but that she won't act on it. She gets more depressed when she stops her medications as she has done on several occasions. She states she won't harm herself and that she will call someone if she gets intrusive thoughts again.

Plan- discharge her today at vets request- continues to request discharge despite recommendations for continued treatment.

/es/ Lisa Hammers

M.D.

Author Note: It is hard to admit when you get to the point that you need help. It is even harder to admit that you want to kill yourself.

I was tired and sick and unhappy with how my life had turned out. Suicide seemed an option because if you were asleep forever you wouldn't have the nightmares anymore or pain.

## Chapter

# 6

**Progress Notes**  February 24, 2005

Met with female veteran x 90 min today

EMDR session focused on MST. Veteran tolerated the process well and was able to verbalize recognition that "I did my best". I reinforced this positive cognition several times.

Requested she keeps a journal of any new information or thoughts and bring to next session. She said she thought that would be a good idea.

Will scheduled appointment when she knows her schedule for March.

/es/ Kristi Olsen

MSW

Author note: I don't keep a journal sort of like I don't like to read books.

Surprisingly, I enjoyed the EMDR.

This allowed me to unblock some of the images that I have repressed. The main image that I was able to regain was of being choked. I had always assumed that it was the sergeant chocking me but it was me. I had tried to lift my body up off the bed but, I was not strong enough to lift myself and him off of me so, my hands got stuck under my throat and I was choking myself.

## Progress Notes                                June 23, 2005

Met with female veteran x 60 min

Female veteran brought in all of the paper work that she had sent to the VA Adjudication Board to talk about her experience. The documentation in the record is vague to this point due to the female veteran's unwillingness or inability to talk about specifics (which were honored by the trauma providers). She rambled as she talked, became increasingly anxious to the point of talking in a high pitched voice. Deep breathing exercises were practiced before continuing.

She provided actual records that she had collected; a denial from the Adjudication Board; a lack of understanding of the rationale of why anyone needed to know any of this in more depth then she had already given; and still resistive to providing more information. So this ACSW and patient began going through her records to pull out those experiences that she was attempting to identify related to her traumatic experience, began to spell out some of her vagueness in the words she used and lack of descriptive behavior to support those labels such as "harassment" vs "sexual harassment:, "attacked vs actual behavior", verbal threats vs perception and fear from actual behavior all of which she was still somewhat resistive to explaining or defining specifically, rape, so the session was an echoing & reflecting of her words asking what she meant or what the actions had been that she perceived as threatening or warranting fear.

She was finally able to get to the following descriptive behavior as not documented prior:

Veteran was able to discuss an incident that happen while she was on a mission "we were at a pool and the sergeant put me at "parade rest" in front of civilians and my daughter; he walked around me and made derogatory comments and ogling me"

The incident she describes of Jan. or Feb. of 1991 during a mission. She goes on to say "nobody listen to me when we were back at the unit and I feel as if nobody listens to me now" "I called the next person in line of authority who sat down with the Sargent and me, the outcome of that conference was that he was to stay away from her, but were left on the same mission because of how short the unit was of men because, everyone was in Dessert Storm."

This session had gone on for one hour so was stopped with some relaxation exercises; some better understanding of why the information was so important.

/es/Janet Drapper

L.C.S.W.

Author Note: Parade rest is when your superior makes you stand with your hands behind your back and you can't move.

First of all the sergeant was drunk, cause I could smell the alcohol. Second, he walked around me making fun of my boobs, my butt, my stretch marks-how he could see them and that I should cover them up. I was humiliated in front of civilians and, not to mention the concern I had for my daughter watching all of this.

Really, this was not happening but sure enough it did. I have struggled with my body image. I refuse to wear a 2 piece- always a one piece with a shirt over it in case someone saw my stretch marks.

The pressure of that mission was too much at this time –I called back to the unit but most of the higher ranking officers were in

Dessert Storm so, I had to let whoever was at the desk know what was happening. I did not hear back from the First Sargent for a whole day, during that time I was terrified to go out by the pool.

After, the First Sargent called, the Sargent was to leave me alone and only talk to me when we were at the office. He didn't leave me alone, I was hoping that they would have called him off the mission, but I was wrong again.

One of the problems I still have is that I feel nobody is listening to me. I feel if I yell and scream nobody can hear me. I go to the doctor and tell them no-one is listening to me, they are listening to me but I feel in my soul that if the Army would have just paid attention to my plea for help I would not have this constant fear of not being heard.

## Progress Notes                                          June 10, 2005

Met with female veteran x 30 min

I haven't seen this veteran since October but she was hospitalized earlier this year with worsening depression and suicidal thoughts. She reports many different physical problems. Diagnosed with Lupus, she report daily depression and occasional bouts of hopelessness but does contract for safety and denies any more active plan of suicide at this time. She quit her job at the Vets Home and now is a house monitor 3 days a week.

She denies use of alcohol or drugs(note that there was a time she was cautioned about her use of alcohol) She is not sleeping well, she denies any side effect from the venlafaxine and queries whether she might need a higher dose to which I respond in the affirmative.

Objective: anxious, appropriately groomed, externalizing women; affect labile, mood depressed and anxious, denies suicidal ideation; rational, no Delusions or hallucinations present, sensory is clear

/es/ Daniel Swartz MD

Author Note: Had just quit the Vet's home. I walked out, not something I am proud of. The Vets Home had done a couple of shitty things 1. I had my boss tell me to stop talking about lupus because apparently I talked about Lupus too much. 2. Another lady that worked there got discoid Lupus and all of a sudden everyone talked about it and still I wasn't allowed to say shit about Lupus. 3. After, being harassed by the head housekeeper- now this – I have had enough.

The stress of my daughter graduating from high school was really hard because I felt, like all parents, that I was losing my best friend. This was difficult; I would miss our long talks at night with her sitting at the end of my bed, our cry time with raw chocolate cookie dough. Her corky sense of humor and her intelligence that I love. I always relied on her. This was a big mile stone for her and me.

## Progess Notes June 15, 2005

Met with female veteran today x 50 min

She reports episodes of depression since the military (1992); her depression has been ongoing and she has gotten treatment.

Panic attacks have occurred since the military and the incident with her superior at the swimming pool. She reports that her panic attacks, her breathing becomes rapid to the point that her chest hurts and her hands tremble.

She reportedly has had more than 32 jobs since she left the military and had not stayed in a job if she did not like it or if in any confrontation at the job. The longest she ever stayed at a job was at the VAMC here in Sheridan. She began having more panic attacks in her last year working at the Vets Home where she felt harassed, made complaint in the form of a grievance, lost about 40lbs, finally walked off of job due to her perception of personal injustices to her.

Events that happened in the military have affected me dramatically.

"I was afraid to go to the infirmary, so I did not see a medical person "The nightmares didn't start right away they only started when I was in Germany. I would get the "evil dream" when I woke up I was paralyzed and unable to move, unable to breath and was afraid I was going to die. I then went to see a counselor."

Today she reports the recurring nightmares, unable to move, unable to breathe. She has anxiety attacks that cause her chest to hurt.

She has sought out medical & mental health treatment, and has made an initial effort to get psychiatric treatment since no physical etiology was found.

PTSD

Complete MST paper work

/es/ Janet Drapper

L.C.S.W.

Author Note: I have had a lot of jobs over the years. I get overwhelmed and I quit. I sought out medical/psychiatric treatment because I knew I needed help I could no longer do it on my own. My feelings have always been private so seeking the help I needed was difficult.

In many ways, I spent a lot of time fighting that help. I would only talk about the things I was comfortable talking about with others. This was events/life that I felt I was able to reveal while still not revealing what the true problems were.

## Progress Notes                                August 31, 2005

Met with female veteran x 50 min today

Veteran seems anxious when she arrives today, says "I hate coming up here and I get anxious when I have to be here." Reports that she has had severe panic attacks in the past months and wants help to resolves whatever is triggering the attacks. After some discussion about probable triggers she concludes that the stress of a low paying job and Lupus being main factors in panic attacks.

Discussed options for coping with these triggers which would be beneficial

/es/ Kristi Olsen

MSW

Author Note: I have a lot of triggers and I have just realized that is what is affecting my anxiety and continued depression. Coming to the VA causes panic attacks for me cause (1) I know I will have to talk about things I don't want to talk about. (2) The VA is a constant reminder of the Army. (3) The fucking doorways! These remind me of the time when the SGT. forced his way into my room.

## Progress Notes                                November 10, 2005

Met with female veteran x 15 min

39 year old vet came into office and was quite angry and said she did not want to talk, that she was pissed off with the doctors who are always telling her everything is in her head. I tried to get her to open up a bit and give me more info but she declined saying she just wanted to leave and did not want any more f—king meds. There was no evidence that she was in danger to self or others.

angry, disheveled woman, will not provide any information to me, passive aggressive, no eye contact, mood depressed rational, sensorium is not clouded.

/es/

Daniel Swartz MD

Author Note: The VA doctors think everything is PTSD and that nobody has a physical issue. The doctors are always thinking it has to be a mental disorder and then there are those that just want to give you drugs to make the problem go away. Well when the drugs are not working, it is obvious that it is not mental and is indeed physical. Drugs are not the fucking answer to everything!

## Progress Notes                                November 10, 2005

Met with female veteran x 50 min

Veteran says her primary care provider has tried to explain to her that the chest pain is a result of her anxiety. "I just don't understand how my brain can cause my chest to hurt" She was not receptive to any further explanation of anxiety and chest pain. I Suggested that she do some research at the library about anxiety and the physiological implications of prolonged anxiety. I was able to get her to talk about the benefits and consequences of resolving the anger. Benefits of the behavior, she admits that being angry allows her not to take responsibility for her behavior; may be attention seeking; allows her to isolate, and serve as a "protection". She verbalizes recognition that the consequence of her behavior includes, being childish in her demands of others; causes chest pain; interferes with employment, being overweight. Benefits of letting go of the anger; no chest pain, better employment opportunities, more outgoing, have more energy.

After this exercise, she states the desire to "get better". I discussed her willingness to work toward the goal of resolving her anger issues.

/es/ Kristi Olsen

MSW

Author Notes: I know why I am angry. The events in my past have contributed a lot to the anger I feel each day. I have days that I don't feel anger. It takes small things to trigger my anger; several times I have jumped to anger before thinking about it. I am ashamed to have to admit it but, I do have anger issues.

My chest hurts because of anxiety and I personally kept on telling the Doctors that it was physical not mental-I found out that it was mental later- apparently I'm really stubborn.

## Progress Notes April 05, 2006

Met with Female veteran x 30 min

I haven't seen this veteran for a while and last time was upset; she is generally better now. Vet is somatically preoccupied and we discussed this; she has had headaches and believes that maybe the lupus is the problem. I noted to her that her labs and sed rate were normal, Vet denies any suicidal ideation.

Cooperative, spontaneous, verbal, affect labile, mood depressed not markedly so and no suicide ideation elicited; rational

Ptsd, non-combat, depression

increase venlafaxine and social therapy

/es/ Daniel Swartz MD

# Chapter

# 7

**Progress Notes**  March 16, 2007

PSYCHIATRIC ADMISSION EVALUATION NOTE

40 yr old female veteran

"I can't take the pain anymore" Has been feeling horrible for three days. She noticed getting sick on Monday, made her mixed connective tissue disease worse.

"Much pain can't sleep, very tired, very depressed"

Was only hospitalized one day (psychiatric) in the past? Is on venlafaxine now, and has been trying to stop taking it since she feels it contributes to her weight gain.

Child hood: Billings, MT "it was ok" "normal"

Education: Sophomore in college

Military: Army 87-89, 89-92, 93-95.

Social: 3 children, divorced, 2 children live with her

Legal: none

mixed connective tissue disease, unspecified muscle disease

Very distraught, tearful and overwhelmed with pain, sadness and anxiety, no si, but can see how someone might feel at this point. Sleep is poor, fragmented and restorative. Her main motif is helplessness and pain.

Axis I- autoimmune disease, PTSD, non-combat

Axis II- Depression

Axis III Chronic pain

Plan: Admit to unit 8

Fortify pain regimen

/es/ Matt R. Reise MD

Author Note: Yup! Another trip to Unit 8, I have a new Doctor-he's weird. I don't feel well and the anxiety is uncontrollable with my chest hurting and freezing up. Found out that it was fiber myalgia and that it really was all in my head. Not something I wanted to face or own up too but it is what it is.

## Progress Notes                                         March 19, 2007

Met with female veteran x 20 mins in rounds

"Flare up with pain, my daughter will help me, pain management clinic; I'm going to file for social security."

Speech and thought coherent, mood and affect depressed and anxious

Depression, major, PTSD, non-combat, patient has been talking to staff about discharge and leaving, MST issues, Patient demanding to leave at present

Continue on meds, follow up with coping skills to see Dr. Drapper, MST issues, pain management, Discharged for home.

/es/ Matt Reise MD

Author Note: I don't particularly like this Doctor he is quite the character. When you sit at his desk to talk with him his desk is full of water bottles, all sorts of cups too. Some bottles full of soda pop, some full of coffee and others full of juice and then there are some half full. This is very distracting- I mean there are at least 20-30 water bottles-personally I think this guy needs help more than me and that's saying a lot!

## Progress Notes                    March 26, 2007

Met with female veteran x 50 min

Veteran talked about feeling "overwhelmed" with pain and her limitations due to physical problems. Believes she can't take care of hardly any task, and is angry about this. I suggested pain management techniques, including imagery and hypnosis, with explanation of how they can help. She says she has a relaxation tape but has not been using it. I asked her to practice with this tape twice daily. She describes pain as "burning", and "twitching", with extreme muscle tightness. Stress increases her symptoms. We did a short imagery practice today, focusing on visualizing her muscles and helping them to release the pain. She was able to do this, and I asked her if she could do this at home and she expressed willingness to do so. We also did some cognitive work, addressing her MST issues.

/es/ Les Smith PHD

Psychologist

Author note: The pain is unmanageable, chronic pain is horrible and unless you experience it no – one will understand it! I was having major pain and it was un bearable.

## Progress Notes                                        April 14, 2007

Met with female veteran x 20 min

She needs some meds refilled, depression is ok. Veteran stated that "I need to get the pain under control", "My muscles are squeezing me" She has a lot of muscle spasms, hard to do daily activities. She is listening to relaxation tapes which are helping. Money seems to be issue " son had to give can of food to food pantry for extra credit at school veteran told son not to worry will pick can up again when she goes back to food pantry"

Female veteran also upset about having to switch from one DR to another, one social worker to another, explain to her that people have retired or moved. She accepts this explanation. She also makes rude comment about the amount of drinking glasses on my desk.

Mood and affect depressed and anxious

PTSD, non-combat, major depression

Continue meds and return for follow up

/es/ Matt Reise MD

Authors note: So I was rude, what's the big deal?? I know, bitch moment.

Also, my family still laughs about how we gave the school a can of food we just picked up from the food pantry, and then picked it back up the next day. My son got extra credit that's all that matters.

## Progress Notes                                    May 5, 2007

Met with female veteran x 30 min

Patient states that "the meds seem to be working for depression" she was told that if she became depressed again that she should attend the smile program. She just had a sleep study done and has to wear a cpap mask. She says that she doesn't like the mask or doorways because of her MST. The more we talk the more she becomes reluctant to talk about incident in the Army. Patient states she "has issues"

PTSD, Depression, MCTD, Energy, motivation, and concentration are good, speech and thought coherent, mood and affect anxious, feel ok mentally.

/es/ Matt Reise MD

Psychiatrist

Authors Note: I don't like this doctor and prefer he take his drinking problem and leave the VA and go somewhere else!!! I will not talk to someone whom I don't trust, trust this guy, come on?

## Progress Notes                                    July 24, 2007

Met with female veteran x 30 min

Significant issues, symptoms, complaints: veteran is currently on Effexor for depression. She reports it is not working and wants a different anti-depressant. She is currently depressed about being denied SSI but is going to try again this time with an attorney. I do not see evidence of a thought disorder.

She is constantly worried about what the future will be like for her medically, is under a treatment of a doctor whom she sees monthly. Veteran also worried about finances.

In the past Zoloft which was not helpful, her depression seems to be connected to her medical problems, veteran is also a 30% service connected. Her symptoms of depression include being tearful and sad. She denies being suicidal and she is not homicidal, she denies any hallucinations.

I strongly recommend therapy but she is reluctant to talk about MST issue suggested that getting the incident out in the open we can better help her.

Assessment- will start her on celexa; we discussed the medication and side effects.

Plan- will do follow up

/es/ Cindy Liner MD

Author Note: Another doctor, can you imagine me not opening up? I really can't stand this. Have to start over each time with a new doctor, I am tired of it! Can't they just read my notes and continue from there? Yes, my depression is worse and I can tell you it had a lot to do with not being able to work, hurting all the time, not having any money to do anything, grrrrrr who wouldn't get depressed? Fucking idiots - what the fuck- so sick of this switching doctor shit I could just scream!

## Progress Notes                                          August 27, 2007

Met with female veteran x 30 min

Female veteran has had anxiety attacks from age 30 or so .... Hard to tell freq- maybe once every few weeks - always reassured not heart attacks. Has realized that they have been panic attacks, but still goes in when chest pain gets to be too much. Heart rate goes up, and so does Blood pressure, but she does not check herself.

In the last year has gone twice – one was about a month ago and one in July.

Not taking flexeril now does have some relief from the primidone- got on these a few months ago from neurologist. Still gets occasional muscle squeezing (daily several times, only for few seconds); used to have these all day Neurologist diagnosed them as myoclonic jerks.

Not employed now. Last time was over a year ago. Quit due to medical and psychiatric reasons. Sensitive

Denver Rheumatologist has seen her twice and he does not know what she has that would cause all of these- not lupus

Typical day; drives son to seminary LDS, sometimes gets exercise, sometimes not, then cleans house – takes a nap and then watches TV rest of day.

She has sleep apnea and should be on cpap, but she can't relax enough to fall asleep with it

Urged her to use her cpap. And will give her something that will help with that.

/es/ Matt R. Reise MD

Authors note; The VA finally sent me to a neurologist after 2 fucking years. I am pissed off. I have told them and told them that something was wrong with me and that my muscles were squeezing me and it felt as though my bones were going to break. I would think if someone told you this that they would probably rule out neurological but noooooo. 2 fucking years I suffered with this and they wonder why I have such trust issues with the VA.

I am pleased that I got on primidone because my life is 100% better. My left hand still shakes but the doctors have told me it is from PTSD. I have come to accept the fact that my left hand shakes, but it is embarrassing when I have to take a drink or hand someone something, so I try not to do it.

Yes, I have joined the Church of Jesus Christ of Latter Day Saints. I am very pleased with my decision and feel it is the best thing I have ever done! I love my church and believe this has a lot to do with my recovery. I joined in December of 2006. My son became friends with a member and we started to take lessons and shortly thereafter we were baptized into the Church of Jesus Christ.

Now don't get me wrong but I have 40 years of cussing in me and it is hard to get rid of that potty mouth. My son has charged me a dollar for each cuss word and he swears that's how he paid for his college.

One time in church I was giving my testimony and was explaining how I owed my son 50 dollars for the potty mouth. I'll never forget the look on the lady in the front row – she has never come visit me at home. Hah!

# Chapter 8

**Progress Notes**  April 3, 2008

Met with female veteran x 30 min (walk in)

Veteran has a lot of emotions coming up, wonders about coming into hospital.

Feels angry, hates men now

Mood-depressed

/es/ Tom Neilson MD

Authors Note; another fucking doctor! I guess they get burnt out on all of this depressed bullshit.

I suppose I would probably get burnt out too. I would tell the patients to shut up and get a life, but then I think it's hard to get a life when you hurt all the time and your stuck in trauma of the past and no way to get past it. I'm such a bitch!

**Progress Notes**                    **August 1, 2008**

Met with female veteran x 35 min

This is the first time meeting with this veteran. It appears the veteran was mostly seen by a mental health prescriber in early April of this year. The note from that meeting was reviewed and appreciated. Veteran opened session by stating "my Neurologist wants me back on antidepressants. Veteran talked today about health issues which cause chronic pain and which she feels has decreased her quality of life.

This clinician inquired what symptoms of depression are most problematic. Veteran says that she cries easily which is apparent during the session. Also she feels sad much of the time. After talking with veteran this sadness may have a grief component. Veteran is just 42 years old but physical problems have resulted in some significant losses. Veteran denies suicidal ideation or intent.

Female veteran came for this session casually dressed in clean clothes. Initially she was defensive but this seemed to resolve some as session progressed, Veteran feels she has been disregarded by medical and mental health providers who have seen her in the past because her symptoms are complicated and difficult to treat. Veteran has admitted that it is frustrating for her when she feels that others do not believe her about her symptoms.

Complicating her case is she has a history of Military Sexual Trauma which is related to a rape. Veteran is reluctant to talk of incident. Veteran made good eye contact as we talked today.

Anxiety, PTSD, major depressive disorder

Effexor increases to 150 mg a day follow up in one month

/es/ Loree Bourdoex

Mental Health Nurse Practitioner

Authors Note; I am very depressed right at this point in my life, seems I can't get a grip on reality, going to church has helped me a lot and I really enjoy church and I feel that this has been the only reason at this point in my life to not give up and commit suicide. Thank-you Jesus!

## Progress Notes                    August 19, 2008

Met with female veteran today x 30 min

Veteran came for the session casually dressed in clean clothes; her hygiene and grooming were good. She was more open with sharing information today than when this clinician initially saw her. She avoided sustained eye contact. Her self-confidence seemed somewhat low. Mood seemed both depressed and anxious. There was no evidence of psychosis. Veteran was alert and oriented and cooperative with answering questions. She denies suicidal ideation or intent.

Posttraumatic stress disorder complicates this case. Veteran has MST issues while in the service. This happened while on a mission in Texas, she was subsequently transferred to Germany, where she developed nightmares. PTSD symptoms became so distressing that she reportedly intentionally got herself pregnant so that she could get discharged from the service. Veteran says as a result of the pregnancy out of wedlock, she was rejected her mother. Veteran was involved in therapy with MST counselor here at Sheridan VAMC starting in 2000 and ending in 2005.

Anxiety, PTSD Major Depression disorder

Veteran is too continue with antidepressants and encourages coming in for therapy

/es/ Loree Bourdoex

Mental health Nurse Practitioner

Authors Note; I was married to someone else when I got pregnant, yes, that's true but what the Cheyenne VA didn't put in the report was that I tried to change duty stations, I tried to get out on hardship and I couldn't get out!

I can only express myself in this way, I was desperate and I wanted out! I was scared, nightmares constantly. I honestly thought the barracks I lived in were haunted. CRAZY!

I decided to get pregnant because I knew I could get out that way. Sure enough, was pregnant within a month. My plan was to get out of the Army, go home, get an abortion, and get on with life. Well God had a different plan, I couldn't go through with the abortion and I am glad I didn't. My son has been a blessing to me and to our family and I love him.

As far as my mother is concerned wouldn't you be pissed off if your daughter came home from the Army pregnant with her third child, all different fathers, and getting her third divorce?

I love my mother and she is a great mother!!!!!

## Progress Notes                    November 03, 2008

Met with female veteran x 30 min

Female veteran expressed a lot of frustration today. This was primarily directed toward specialists who have been evaluating her related to a possible diagnosis of lupus. She used foul language and was tearful when expressing her anger and frustration toward specialists who have been seeing her. She seemed ashamed as she shared her perception that medical staff who work with her see her as "a basket case" veteran admitted that she is having hard time coping with things. This clinician has met with veteran twice previously and her presentation at our previous sessions has been considerably calmer and more controlled.

Female veteran reported that chronic pain is adding to her stress. She said that the pain is so bad at night that she is sometimes unable to sleep. This clinician recommended that she goes down to primary care and talk with one of her doctors about her concerns.

Veteran is dealing with several stressors; her 21 year old daughter is having surgery next month due to some tumors that need to be removed that are affecting her hearing. Veteran's father was hospitalized and, this last month she had to deal with a situation with her son where a classmate had threatened to kill him. This clinician inquired whether veteran has been feeling suicidal or whether she is currently suicidal veteran states" I really wish I could, I'll be honest with you, but I won't because my children need me", also veteran is Latter Day Saint and her religion would prohibit this behavior.

PTSD Chronic, Major depression disorder

A number of stresses seemed to have combined to overwhelm veterans coping skills and she behaved today as though in crisis. She was allowed to express her anger; however, because of her level of distress, this clinician requested she see the on-call psychiatrist. Veteran was reluctant about this but eventually agreed to do so. Veteran did not meet with on-call psychiatrist. Female veteran did call this afternoon and told receptionist that she arrived home safe and "all is well".

This clinician offered veteran valium for short term use during this period of time when she is feeling so overwhelmed. Veteran declined stated" I don't want to become an addict"

This clinician offered to make a referral to the outpatient therapist and suggested that veteran might see her on short term basis during this difficult period of time, but veteran refused. This clinician will contact veteran by phone early next week to enquire how she is doing.

/es/ Loree Bourdoex

Mental Health Nurse Practitioner

Authors Note; ugh! That's all I got to say about this period of my life.

I also want to mention that giving drugs out to veterans is not always the answers. They are always giving out fucking medicine, here take this pill, it'll shut you up and no we don't have another way of dealing with what you are going through even though, I have a degree and spent thousands of dollars on education. Now be a good solider and take your fucking pill.

**Progress Notes**                                **November 12, 2008**

Met with female veteran x 30 min

Veteran is more composed today than when this clinician saw her last week. She was not tearful or tremulous. She did not behave as though she were feeling overwhelmed. She seemed to be dealing with her frustrations and stresses a lot better. She talked about entering the PCOD program.

Veteran reports a history of sexual trauma, a rape by a superior, her, sergeant. Veteran has been seen by MST counselor here at the Sheridan VAMC. Starting in October 2000 and ending in July 2005. Veteran's initial session with the MST counselor was documented: she finally concluded that the origin of her sexual trauma was not from the military; however, with counseling she apparently did not feel comfortable at first to fully disclose what happen due to fear. It is difficult for her to talk about rape in which this clinician has noted. In the session of 2005 the MST counselor diagnosed PTSD and was helping veteran. Female veteran completed paper work for related to MST/PTSD from the military.

Female veteran stated today that she feels that she needs help related to the MST; "I do not seem to be able to move on from this thing by myself" Female veteran was just remarried and has been finding herself waking up at night time fighting her husband. She finds it difficult to hug others including her children.

Veteran came to session casually dressed in clean clothes. Her hygiene and grooming were good. Veteran made eye contact as we talked; although uncomfortable discussing past trauma of MST, she kept her composure and remained focused. The female veteran thinking is logical and organized. She exhibited a sense of humor during our session. She was neither tearful nor distraught as at our session a week ago. She denies Suicidal thoughts or intent. She is a Mormon and stated that she would not take her own life.

PTSD, major depressive disorder

Will increase venlafaxine by 37.5 mg

Veteran took application today for the PCOD program. Veteran was encouraged to seriously consider treatment in this residential program.

/es/ Loree Bourdoex

Mental Health Nurse Practitioner

Authors Note; Not sure about the PCOD program, but thought it would help me get past this PTSD and forward with my life. I have never been to therapy and didn't know what to expect but I was excited to see if will help.

I remarried in June of 2008. I thought I would give it another shot- can't give up on love right?

*Chapter*

# 9

PTSD & Co. Occurring Disorders (PCOD) Program

Mental Health Note: This Female Veteran was processed onto unit 6R at 1000 hrs Female Veteran will be boarding at the domiciliary.

/es/ Tess fellows

Counseling assistant

**Signed;** 03/19/2009
---

Mental Health Note: Female veteran arrived to appointment with Psychology Technician on time on 3/20/09 @ 1000 hrs Administered the Shipley and MMPI2 to veteran according to test procedures. Veteran completed the test in 95 min.

Response: Veteran read test instructions, verbalized her understanding of them, and completed the test. She was pleasant and actively participated in testing.

Plan: provide Veteran's psychologist with test results for interpretation.

/es/ Greg Neilson

Authors Note; So Happy to be in therapy, I just can't wait to get started and learn how to manage life and get past this trauma.

**Signed;** 3/20/2009

Mental Health Note: This is only a partial assessment, will complete it tomorrow.

42 year old White Female 30% Service connected for physical issues, disabled (denied from social security), divorced x 5, married now, has 16 year old son still at home.

Female veteran has long term problems with depression and anxiety, physical difficulties with pain, in the context of difficulty coping with her problems.

Female veteran states" I shake all the time, I can't eat, I can't brush my teeth all they tell me is I have a chemical imbalance in my head, and I'm very tired "I joined the LDS religion and that's pretty much enlightened me spiritually, I believe there is something wrong with me physically and nobody believes me, I feel the same as I did in the military when I kept telling them that the sergeant was harassing me." I asked her if she thought she was crazy and she states "I 'am crazy, just a little" but aren't we all "Veteran also states that since she moved in the Dom she has recurring nightmares "the place reminds me of the Army".

Stressors prior to the military—"I didn't have any, my first husband was kind of abusive", "a few small things from childhood "but nothing major": there were 5 children in the home.

Stressors during the military—"I didn't have any until that last year, I enjoyed it, I actually wanted to stay in", she was stationed in Texas and a particular Sgt was in charge of her " it didn't matter what I did, it was always horrible' and he would pull her into his office " and ask me stupid questions like" why do you people go to the bathroom in the middle of the night and not flush the toilet?" once he put her at parade rest in the middle of a swimming pool "and he walked around me and commented on every little detail of my body—and my daughter was sitting there…and civilians", I couldn't roll up the wire right.. I couldn't command the lower ranking individuals in our group right." He put me at parade rest all the time… I finally turned him in, and nobody listened to me cause nothing was done… and then we got called into the first sergeants office and asked if we could get along for a mission that was coming up, and I said yes, just because I wanted it so bad –it was to be my first mission and I really wanted it." IT WAS THE SWEETEST JOB EVER! We got a hotel room, a rental car, TDY pay and to top it off I got to keep my daughter with me all I had to do every day was show up and keep records of drug interdiction".

When female veteran came back from mission she had issues from the MST." I went on leave hoping I would feel better when I got back; I got orders to go to Germany. I started to have nightmares shortly after arriving there. I thought my barracks was haunted because they were WWII barracks and I went to the Chaplin and told him about the "evil" dream and he told me it wasn't the barracks that I need to talk to mental health because what happened on the mission. He sent me to Mannheim Mental Health Clinic. The military wouldn't let me come home, I tried everything, change of duty, hardship, and finally I just got pregnant and came home. My first thought was that I would get an abortion, but I couldn't go through with that."

Veteran states" that job after job, I couldn't hold one down, I was always poor, never had any food, for crying out loud I went to a garage sale and put things on layaway, how funny is that, it came up to about ten dollars, we still laugh about that."

Assessment: Essentially normal neurological examination in a lady who has marked anxiety reactions; she admits to having phobias but does not want to talk about it or seek out any psychological counseling, it should be noted that this fine tremor she shows me is not a resting tremor; it is more of an intentional tremor,

Axis I Depression, PTSD

Axis II none

Axis III SLE Lupus

Axis IV moderate sever - health

Axis V Admission 55

/es/ Cathy Wilkerson

M.D. Psychiatrist

**Signed;** 3/24/2009

---

Authors Note; WOW! The light of the third degree is still burning on my face. Geeees, feel like I was cornered and given an enema to answer those questions. Ugh, thought this would be easier but it's not. This doctor asked a lot of questions concerning the mission I went on and what happen. I ended up telling her a lot more than what I was comfortable talking about.

The dorm where I am staying is causing some serious anxiety, there are guys that are staying down the hall and I know there is a monitor but it still feels threating. I do not like therapy!!!

Mental health Group Note

Female veteran is a 42 year old who comes to Mental Health Recovery group as part of ongoing mental health treatment.

24: Number of patients in attendance.

50: minutes with patients.

General focus of group:

After a check in with the group on welfare the veteran was to learn and commit to thinking in terms of models where "Spirituality" that would be significant to the understanding and application for managing mental health.

Patient's Goal:

The veteran's goals are to relate to and apply those aforementioned concepts with regard to her mental health issues.

Progress made:

The veteran seemed to engage with the information given.

Behavior of patient:

The veteran's mood was good with congruent affect.

/es/ Rob Jennings

Psychologist

**Signed;** 03/25/2009

Psychology Admission Assessment:

Female veteran was given the Shipley Institute of Living Scale and the MMPI-2 on 3/19/09 as part of admission assessment. The following are the results.

Shipley Scale   Standard Score Percentile

Verbal 45 31

Abstract        58      79

Clinical Quotient      100 --

Abstract Quotient*     115     --

Wais Estimate 100

Note: * Abstract Quotient is the Clinical Quotient adjusted for age. CQ scores

Shipley Results:

Intellectual Functioning; Within Normal Limits.

MMPI-2 Results:

This is a classic PTSD profile that is accurate, consistent and significantly elevated indicating severe depression, anxiety and estrangement. The veteran wants to see herself as functioning better than her manifest history would predict. Consequently she may have strong motivation to work on recovery, especially if one formulates her clinical tasks in terms of leading from strengths, engaging her in solution-based exercises, and, in short, bypassing discussions of impairment, suicidal history and psychopathology.

/es/ Rob Jennings

Psychologist

**Signed;** 03/27/2009

Mental Health Group Note

Female veteran is a 42 year old veteran who comes to the PTSD Group as part of ongoing mental health treatment.

13: Number of patients in attendance.

50: minutes spent with patients

General focus of group:

Anger management

Behavior of patient;

Actively involved in group.

Referral Diagnosis for group; PTSD

/es/ Sam Mallory, Ph. D.

**Signed;** 03/30/2009

Mental Health Note

Female veteran came to Unit 6 at 2015 hrs.' and asked if this writer had time to talk to her about several things that have been bothering her lately. Vet shared that she was having a hard time with feelings of being worthless and that there had been several incidents last week and today with other veterans and several hospital staff that had resulted in her becoming angry and questioning why she was here at all. Veteran was tearful and angry at different times during our conversation. It was recommended that she talk to both her doctor and case manager about conflicting feelings that she was having.

/es/ David Wilson Counselor

**Signed;** 03/31/2009

Authors Note; There have been some incidents that have bothered me and the main one is the mental health workers in this program have decided that someone with Military Sexual Trauma would be ok to sit in a dark room with combat men. The mental health workers would put in a movie, turn the lights out and walk out and I be the only female in a darken room with combat veterans. Really what were they thinking???? I do not have combat issue's I have Military Sexual Trauma issues and this act has caused me some serious anxiety.

Also, this treatment program is for people with drug and alcohol issue's which I do not have any more, since I joined the Church of Jesus Christ of Latter Day Saints 2yrs ago! However, I do have a coffee addiction, hard to kick the good oh cup of sin.

Mental Health Group Note

Female veteran is 42 year old who came to MHR group as part of ongoing mental health treatment.

23: number of patients

50: Minutes spent with patients.

General focus of group

After a check on the welfare of group the veterans was to learn and commit to thinking in terms of models where "Dual Diagnosis" that would be significant to the understanding and application for managing mental health.

Patient's goals:

The veteran goals are to relate to and apply those aforementioned concepts with regard to her mental health issues.

Progress made:

Veteran seemed to engage with the information given.

Behavior of patient

The veteran's mood was good.

/es/Rob Jennings

Psychologist

**Signed;** 03/31/2009

Mental Health Note

Female veteran is a walk in this am and is upset and angry. She becomes tearful as she shares angry feelings about several recent events that in part relate to her being a female veteran. She is in the PTSD track and we are presently completing the psychosocial assessment.

She will complete psychosocial today with integrated summary and treatment plan to follow. The undersigned consulted with New Women's Veterans program manager as well, who will contact veteran today.

/es/ Sam Mallory, Ph.D.

**Signed;** 03/31/2009

Authors Notes; Once again, let's put in a movie, turn the lights out and see what happens to the girl with sexual trauma does?? Fucking idiots!!! Plus, I DO NOT HAVE ALCHOL problems!!!

Women's Veterans Support Note

At the request of Dr. Mallory, writer saw patient today for a 90 min women's veterans support session addressing concerns and needs.

Writer advised female veteran of visit and assessment of needs and complaints addressed by Dr. Mallory. Female veteran acknowledged her frustration of PCOD program and how she felt she was in the wrong program because "I do not have an alcohol or substance abuse problem". Writer rephrased and continues to probe. "I cannot express my feelings concerning my trauma in a room full of men. I do not feel my needs and rights as a female veteran are properly being treated by making me be in a room surrounded by all men. "Female veteran continues to discuss her dissatisfaction in being here for 10 days and not being present in team meetings or team discussions concerning plan of care. Writer acknowledged understanding.

Female veteran also advised she did not think the VA provided gender specific care she needed and suggested to this writer a meeting where all the females could be present to discuss their needs. Writer advised this was an excellent idea and continued to probe for ways female veteran could be satisfied with treatment process now. Female veteran began to say" how are you going to help me?" Again writer probed for goals and expectations. Female veteran reports "I want to be well". "I want it to all go away."

While female veteran discussed her military sexual trauma she began to cry. "I was so scared. I did not tell anyone until I arrived in Germany because I was just too scared. He was my sergeant and he just kept on harassing me.

Writer validated how scared the patient must have been and encouraged patient to continue talking about her thoughts and feelings. Patient reported once she was in Germany she began to have "thoughts of a ghost being present" in her living quarters and became afraid she would be harmed again. Patient reports "I wanted to go home at this time but they would not let me. They (the military) accused me of being a whore; after all I had several marriages and 2 kids by two different people." Patient continues to say she attempted to kill herself and received care at the Manheim Mental health Facility. Patient acknowledged fair care but states "I just wanted to go home." Patient reports she became pregnant "so they would send me home" by another man other than her husband. Upon arriving back in the US patient reports her mother called her a whore, slapped her, and told her she didn't want anything to do with her or the child.

Patient states she contemplated abortion but felt God calling her to keep this child. Born out of wedlock was a son, which patient states she is very close to. "I saved my son and my child brought me to saving grace." Patient continues to discuss how she joined the LDS Church at her son's urging.

Patient talked about her many relationships and how stupid she was for being in these past relationships and for all of the decisions she made in her life. Writer discussed how we use language and attempted to discourage patients discrediting remarks concerning self. Patient states "I know I'm not stupid "writer again validated patient and encouraged her to use terms such as "I made mistakes in my life" 'I have not made good decisions', etc. Patient acknowledged understanding.

Patient also reports dissatisfaction in the women's History outing. Patient reported several remarks being made from staff such as" why did we go to all the problems of coordinating a movie outing when only two female veterans showed up!" She felt as if 'once again' of not being important.

Female Veteran also discussed her upcoming hearing with DAV in Washington DC and expressed anger and fear with the hearing. Writer acknowledged fear and advised patient she could have any and all of her family present for testimony.

Female veteran denies any self-harm to self or others at this session. However, patient does endorse prior thoughts and attempts of self-mutilation and suicidal ideation to self. Writer's clinical judgment female veteran is at low to medium risk to harm self or others at this time.

Writer would recommended anger management classes, a female therapist for patient to express and explore thoughts and feelings concerning military sexual trauma.

Writer would also recommend, upon completion of Sheridan program. A referral for this veteran to inpatient women's program for PTSD secondary to MST. Programs available include Palo Alto (although this is not the writers first choice), Bay Pines, Fl, or Cincinnati, OH. All programs would like to see patient be in a sustained program prior to inpatient program. Writer is willing to assist with paperwork if appropriate.

/es/ Hedi Taylor

MSW

**Signed;** 04/01/2009

Authors Note; I am so over whelmed right now wish I could just go home but the VA won't let me leave the program. I think someone should have sent me to a women's program instead of this bull shit!

Mental Health Group Note

Female veteran 42 year old who came to PTSD group as part of ongoing mental health treatment

15: Number of patients in attendance.

52: Minutes spent with patients.

General focus of group: departure ceremony, anger management and brief rationale for cognitive processing therapies (CPT) including prolong exposure

Behavior of Patient: Active in the group process. She talked about being sexually harassed by a senior NCO and became tearful as she did so, received much attention and support from other group members after this disclosure.

Referral diagnosis for group: PTSD

/es/ Sam Mallory Ph.D.

**Signed;** 04/01/2009

Authors Note; I really need to get out what happened to me in the Army, it's eating my SOUL up.

Mental Health Group Note

Female veteran 42 years old who comes to PTSD group as part of ongoing mental health treatment.

12: Number of patients in attendance.

50: minutes spent with patients.

General focus of group: After a check in with the group on welfare the veteran was to learn and commit to thinking in terms of models where "cognitive Processing Therapy" that would be significant to the understanding and application for managing mental health.

Patient Goal(s): The veteran's goals are to relate to and apply those aforementioned concepts with regard to her mental health issues.

Progress made: The female veteran dismissed herself from the group session

Behavior of patient: The veteran became distracting when she burst into laughter after a diagram of a barometer became amusing to her. When asked what was so funny she said "it looks like a dick". The female veteran continued to laugh becoming more of a distraction to the group. Once acknowledged a diversionary tactic was utilized without success. The therapist said, "The other PTSD therapist would not think it was so funny" and the veteran said "bullshit". As she was leaving in anger she pointed out that she wasn't afraid of me and that I was an "arrogant asshole".

/es/ Rob Jennings

Psychologist

**Signed;** 04/02/2009

Authors Note; I have some serious angry emotions right now and I am losing it!!!!!

Mental Health Team Note

PCOD rounds, case manager and peer support present. Female veteran has been taking clonidine0.05 mg in the am and taking 0.2 mg at night. She had 0.1 mg clonidine today after bout of getting upset in class and it calmed her down. She was having nightmares.

She talked today about today's incident in class. She wonders "why did I have to embarrass this poor guy" referring to the instructor "why couldn't I hold back" "why did I have to laugh like that". She says "I just lost it".

42 year old white female with chronic PTSD/MST, depression, anxiety, difficulty with somatic issues, Poor coping skills lately, had a problem today in class.

She is willing to start perphenazine on a regular basis, this may help her feel calmer and may take the edge off of her anger and prevent the type of problem that happened this morning in class.

The Chaplin has arranged for a bishop from her church to visit on Sunday.

/es/ Cathy Wilkerson

M.D. Psychiatrist

**Signed;** 04/02/2009

## Chapter

# 10

Psychiatric Evaluation

Psychiatry Admission Evaluation Note

Female veteran 42 year old white female 30% Service connection for physical issues, divorced x 5, married now, has 16 year old son living at home.

Female veteran here for long term problems with depression and anxiety, she has physical difficulties with pain, in the context of difficulty coping with her problems.

Here for PCOD but today destabilized in class this morning, left early "I don't think anybody cares" and "I don't understand why that other girl wasn't in class, at least I would have somebody" went to her room and removed the blade from her pill cutter and scratched both inner arms superficially several times, then went to the peer support office and was taken to the mental health clinic for treatment.

She talks about instances since her MST in the service where her needs were not listened to. Talks about how being on the DOM has frightened her, there is a patient she fears, talks about how even seeing the doorways in the buildings triggers her.

At this time we will hospitalize her on Unit 8, inpatient psychiatry, for stabilization and reworking her treatment plan.

/es/ Cathy Wilkerson M.D.

Psychiatrist

**Signed;** 04/08/2009

Readjustment Counseling Assistant Note

Female veteran has been temporarily transferred to the Unit 8

I met with this 42 year old white married female in the ward quiet room. She was transferred to ward approx… One hr. ago from the Domiciliary where she was residing while participating in PTSD treatment group.

The diagnosed of record are PTSD secondary to sexual assault while in military service and also depression.

Reason for transfer: PT made 6-8 superficial scratches to both arms using a pill cutter. She described feeling increasing overwhelmed, frustrated, angry, discounted, and isolated in the PTSD program. She reports being extremely uncomfortable and anxious in the groups of men who are for the most part military combat veterans. Patient reports that after 4 weeks she feels she is in a group treatment that is not appropriate for her condition or situation and several times she refers to herself in rather demeaning terms to other group members, such as" I'm not the caliber of these men, they are combat and I'm not". "I have not experienced what they experienced"

Female veteran was direct in saying "your system is broken, why was I put in PTSD program for combat when I have MST issues.

Impression: Female veteran obviously in acute distress, she denies being suicidal and she agrees to let staff know if she feels she needs to cut herself and to talk to staff.

At present, my impression is this VA is counter effective – therapeutic given her intense discomfort with men. She would probably find a women's program more helpful.

/es/ Laura Jennings

Psychologist

**Signed;** 04/08/2009

Psychiatrist Note

Unit 8 rounds

Female veteran 42 year old white female with chronic PTSD/MST, depression, anxiety, difficulty with somatic issues, has had some feelings of guilt about what she did yesterday." I'm so angry, it's in there and it's building and building like a volcano."

Decompensating in the context of being around strangers, especially strange men, feeling her needs have not been listened to for several years. Better today, we developed a plan to continue her in the PTSD program with alterations to make it easier on her; we will discuss it with her case manager when he returns to the office tomorrow to see if it will work.

I will schedule perphenazine 0.5 mg tid, hold if excess sedation, because a low dose of this medication, if tolerated, can help people with emotional liability like this patient.

/es/ Cathy Wilkerson

M.D. Psychiatrist

**Signed;** 04/09/2009

Psychiatrist Note

Unit 8 rounds

Female veteran 42 year old white female with chronic PTSD/MST "I had suicidal thoughts today" "that I wish I had cut deeper, I know I shouldn't have those thoughts". We discussed what she was doing when she had this thought; it was this morning in a bathroom break during class. They were talking about "going away, how people cope and instead of two weeks he stayed away for two months". Her contribution to the discussion was "that I didn't think it was fair that men got to go away when women had to stay home and take care of children and couldn't go away". "I just can't pick up and leave for two weeks or two months, I have responsibilities, guys can do whatever they want… I have to take care of children… I can't just go someplace where I can feel free, I'm trapped". ..Someone told her that her comment was sexist, 'I can't say my feelings in class… I told him to shut up" "I don't know, sometimes my anxiety gets up there really high, and that's when I start to think about killing myself."

She then reported that the glass fell out of her glasses this morning and she thought of using it to cut herself (instead she put it back in the frame).

She has been stopping herself and doing some breathing when she was upset.

I will increase the perphenazine to 1 mg qid.

She and I discussed her level II status given that her thoughts return to self-harm, I will put her back on level I. I will have to order that she can only have her glasses in the big room in front of the nurses.

/es/ Cathy Wilkerson

M.D. Psychiatrist **signed;** 04/10/2009

Authors Notes; yes, was not in my right mind. Yes, I wanted to kill myself, fuck what did they expect out of me? I was raped, and I have emotional problems with the rape. I do want to end my life, I have a miserable life,5 marriages down the tube, 3 kids by 3 different fathers and I can't hold a job down. I'm fucked, who will understand??? You??? No people judge and they will judge me. Fuck you all!!! Fucking Army!!

Women's Veteran's Support Note

Writer visited female veteran on Unit 8 for support due to self-harm and to discuss weekly therapy sessions.

Patient reports that 'Dr. Wilkerson has put me back to level I, she is afraid I will harm myself'. Writer probed for additional information and female veteran reports she is still thinking of self-harm. Writer continued to probe and patient reports 'I could use my glasses. Why didn't I think of that before?' Patient begins to cry and she talks about being tired of everything. Writer directed patient to deep breath validating patient thoughts and redirected her back. Patient stops crying within moments. Female veteran also agreed to contact staff if she should begin to feel like harming herself. Writer will notify the staff concerning statement of using her glasses to harm self.

Patient is concerned what her husband will say about not returning home next week. Writer reframed question and discussed fear associated with husband. Writer encouraged patient to see how much support her husband has been over the last few weeks. Patient acknowledged understanding and confirmed support. Patient gives this writer permission to call husband.

Writer spoke to patient concerning therapy and offered to assist patient with weekly sessions. Patient is appreciative of offer. Writer also advised patient there could not be any specific trauma work started until patient is stabilized. Writer encouraged some DBT skills Training but again advised this would not be started as long as patient is in the locked unit. However, to begin to monitor behaviors and thoughts writer requested patient complete DBT diary Cards nightly. Patient agrees to do so. Writer also encouraged patient to think about her goals for therapy for further discussion next week. Writer will add psychiatrist and other providers to this note.

Writer spoke with patient's husband concerning current situation and goals for treatment. Husband believes 'no one has done anything to help while she has been up there. She is worse now than she was before '. Writer reframed statement and provided education on triggers for PTSD and how treatment sometimes makes symptoms worse for a time. Husband acknowledged understanding. Writer provides writer telephone number and advised husband to contact if he should have any further questions. Husband is appreciative of call.

/es/ Hedi Taylor MSW

**Signed;** 04/10/2009

*Chapter*

# 11

Female veteran comes to PTSD "Seeking Safety" Group as part of ongoing mental health treatment.

13: Number of patients in attendance

54: minutes spent with patients

General focus of Group; "Using Compassion to take back your power" Veterans read practice assignments that included their description of "harsh" vs "compassionate" views of their PTSD and struggles with substance abuse.

Behavior of Patient: Veteran was about 10 minutes late for group. Not unlike previous groups, she became upset and tearful during group and then very apologetic. This solicited much support from nearly all other group members, although somewhat difficult to redirect, she was ultimately cooperative and did not become verbally aggressive.

/es/ Sam Mallory, PH.D.

Supervisor, MHR

**Signed;** 04/10/09

Authors Note; I was embarrassed that I cut my wrist, especially since this was a seeking safety class, so I didn't want to come to class. They made me – fucking doctors- so I apologized to everyone for my actions. God, I hate therapy!

Women's veterans Support Note

Writer met with female veteran and patient's husband/caregiver for 60 mins regarding current care at the Sheridan VAMC. Writer met couple in unit 8.

Care giver begins session by advising of all the people he had spoken with at the VA today. Caregiver voiced frustration with patients care and states he has contacted outside sources for assistance. Writer reframed and provided appropriate support/validation.

Writer continued to probe for additional thoughts and feelings concerning care. Patient acknowledged she had to learn to be aware of her own anger. Writer validated Patient and acknowledged patient does appear to be trying to control and work within proper restraints. Writer also advised patient of her rights as a patient and encouraged patient to voice her concerns in appropriate manner. Patient states "I understand, I'm trying to practice breathing when I feel angry." Writer again validated patient's ability to seek understanding.

Writer provided education on modalities available to patient. Caregiver was upset there is not a MST program. Writer clarified statement advising there is outpatient treatment available but he was correct in stating there was not an inpatient program at this time for females. Patient caregiver voiced his concerns about patient being in room "full of men" to work on MST issues. Writer rephrased and validated concerns. Writer encouraged patient to continue her work while inpatient and to work with MST Coordinator and with this writer. Patient agrees to do so and both agree to continue work as an outpatient. Writer again advised of limited clinical hours and both acknowledged understanding. Writer also provided additional education about PTSD and grief work. Patient states "I had high expectations when I came into the facility. Maybe I was wrong" Writer rephrased and continued to assist in understanding of symptoms.

Patient states she has completed the necessary DBT cards to date and will look forward to sharing with writer on Thursday. Writer validates patient for her work.

Writer appreciates the opportunity to assist this veteran.

/es/ Hedi Taylor

MSW

**Signed;** 04/13/2009

Authors Notes; my husband was very angry with the way I was treated in therapy he even went as far as contacting the Senator and complained. The VA superintendent contacted my husband and set up a meeting. My husband exact words to the VA personal were "Your Damn lucky I didn't contact CNN or nightline on how you have treated her in this program! She was here for help not to be put in a room full of men, shut the lights and pop a movie in! How would you feel if you were in her shoes?" The VA told my husband that sometimes therapy brings up emotions from the past and that's why it is so important to have inpatient programs.

I really don't blame the VA for what I did; they have helped me a lot.

Unit 8 rounds

Met with female veteran x 20 mins

She is seen with her husband present. Denies having suicidal thinking "I had a really good weekend, once I got some sleep" She has not had nightmares for the past few nights. Her husband comments that when she is rested she does well, when she gets tired he says she needs to be go to bed and be left alone. She was using her breathing skills through the weekend, she has used clonazepam 5 x since admission but it makes her groggy.

Re: her PTSD hearing "I don't give a damn about the money! I just want validation to what happen to me-because pretty much they are calling me a whore"

MSE: stable

Gen-in hospital garb, engages easily, and stays with her mature coping manner

No suicide or hallucinations

/es/

Cathy Wilkerson MD

Psychiatrist

**Signed;** 4/13/2009

Authors Notes; YES! I want validation of what happened to me, it shouldn't have happened! Do I want the Military and our government to concede and say yes, this happens all the time, yes! What I want is for someone to hear me when I was in the Army. Why didn't someone put a red flag on him and give him a change of duty or me??? I want to know why they waited so long to help female veterans with Military Sexual trauma and why when we get out of the military there is no place for us to go in the VA system?

Mental Health Group Note

Female veteran comes to the PTSD "seeking safety" group as part of ongoing mental health treatment.

9: number of patients in attendance

50: mins spent with patients

General focus of Group:

We reviewed the definition of both substance abuse and substance dependence. We also discussed, "how substance abuse prevents healing from PTSD". Group members disclosed how the above has impacted their lives.

Behavior of patient: Female veteran was active participant.

Referral diagnosis for group: PTSD

/es/ Sam Mallory Ph.D.

**Signed;** 04/14/2009

Authors Notes; Once again, I DON'T HAVE A DRINKING PROBLEM!!! I'm starting to think I WANT TO HAVE SOME ALCHOL!!!

Psychiatrist Note

Unit 8 rounds - Female veteran said she is exhausted, she feels strongly that there is something wrong with her. "I just want to be heard"

Patient's husband called earlier to ask if he should clear knives or other things out of the house for when she discharges. I asked him to remove the ammunition and the gun but given that she cut herself with a pill cutter blade and has thought about cutting w/her glasses that I do not see that she could be prevented from self-harm with multiple common household items.

42-year old white female with chronic PTSD/MST, depression, anxiety, difficulty with somatic issues. Decompensating in the context of being around strangers, especially strange men, feeling her needs have not been listened to for several years.

Strong tendency to somaticize her anxiety, she is beginning to see that this issue for her where in the past she thought she had an undiagnosed illness.

A note from neurologist notes abnormal involuntary movements of unknown etiology; the report suggested that she has dysmetria of cerebellar origin and a central intention tremor, partially improved on lamotrigine and primidone. It also notes significant anxiety and that this may be exacerbating her tremor.

/es/ Cathy Wilkerson

M.D. Psychiatrist

**Signed;** 04/14/09
___

Authors Notes; my husband, he was so caring that he removed all the knives and guns from the house. Really? The doctor said I could have used anything but he gets an A for trying.

I have come to the conclusion that my tremor, in my fucking left hand, will never go away and have realized that it is from the stress of holding the rape inside of me for so long.

Mental health group note

Female veteran comes to Group as part of ongoing mental health Treatment.

20: number of patients in attendance

50: Minutes spent with patients

General focus of Group:

After a check in with the group on welfare the Veteran was to learn and commit to thinking in terms of models where "models of addiction and Mental Health" that would be significant to the understanding and application for managing mental health.

Progress Made;

Female Veteran seemed to engage with the information given. The Veteran asked interesting and thought provoking questions.

Behavior of patient;

The veteran's mood was good with congruent affect

/es/ Rob Jennings

Psychologist

**Signed;** 04/15/20

*Chapter*

# 12

MST Counseling Consult Note

Met with female Veteran

Female veteran had reported that she tried to address the MST issues on her own and just got more depressed. Today she said, breathing heavily, that she was "just tired….tired of what was happening…tired of whining about it….tired of having my life be such a mess."

History since last seen:

Episodes of depression have continued since she was last seen by this provider in 2005. She reported that she had 2 more jobs since she was last seen (at that time the count was 32). She remarried again in June of 2008 and she said that it was wonderful, he was encouraging to her to get help, he is a ranch hand (formerly a teacher), she also cut both her wrist a week ago "because nobody was listening to me"

She reported had been seen by another MSW for support several times recently.

The alleged sexual assault occurred probably late June, 1991. The female veteran was reminded that she would not talk specifically about the sexual trauma in any of the session in 2005. At this point, she said "I'm so mad that I will tell you everything now." She went on to give the following:

While in the Army she was in a unique unit that put up communications everywhere, like Panama, Korea, anywhere they were needed." I was sent on a mission to Texas for drug interdiction. This was the sweetest mission! You got a rental car, motel room, TDY pay and to top it off- I got to take my daughter! Just make sure I showed up for my job Monday through Friday and that I had daycare for my daughter. Everyone wanted that mission, however the only reason I got it was because everyone was away in Saudi for Dessert Storm. Our commander only took the guys to war he didn't want any females to go. Plus, I was the highest ranking female.

Even before going on the mission I knew this SGT didn't like me. He always harassed me. One time he called me into his office and asked me "why do people go to the bathroom in the middle of the night and not flush the toilet?" What kind of question is that?

One time he kept me outside starting and stopping all the different types of generators for hours, he never did that to any of the other girls. I also got what I thought was frost bite but, turned out to be Renaud's disease. The SGT got mad at me one day for not rolling up the wire right, he was always confrontational. Our platoon went to the barracks' to load and ship out more cameo netting. The other soldiers asked if they can take care of personal things since, we had extra time I said yes. The SGT showed up and asked where they others were and I said they would be down shortly, he put me at parade rest and went on chewing me out for not knowing where my men where, I told him I knew where they were and he threaten to write me up.

One day the 1st SGT called us both in to discuss the mission of Drug interdiction. The first question he asked was could we get along (I had turned him in for harassment several times) I said "yes" as long as he could.

One week later we both were headed for Texas, I was extremely excited because this was my first mission and I got to take my daughter along.

At first everything seem to go just fine, then the SGT wanted to rent an apartment out (one that we would share) that would save us a lot of money, I told him "no"!

I hardly saw him at the office where we worked, but every now and then I would see him at the pool. One evening after work, I ordered pizza and my daughter and I were enjoying the evening eating our pizza when the SGT showed up asked me what I was doing? I said "eating" he got mad at my short answer and demanded I stand at parade rest, while dressed in my swimming suit, the SGT walked around me and laughed at my body for 5 minutes commenting on How thin I was or how fat I was in the butt or how my boobs didn't look good in this swimming suit. In the meantime my daughter was scared and crying because the SGT was yelling at her mom.

I was infuriated with him and afterwards called the unit and spoke with the 1st SGT explaining what had happen he said not to worry he would take care of the problem.

One week later, things seem to be getting better the SGT treated me with a little bit more respect and I thought the worst was over. I was wrong.

One evening my daughter and I were watching TV when there was a knock on the door. The SGT was standing there, so I answered the door – this moment has haunted me ever since.

The SGT slammed the door opened with his hand, smelling of alcohol, He told me that I was prejudiced and that he could prove it and if I had sex with him that would prove I wasn't prejudice otherwise he was going to write me up an article 15. I told him to get out and that is when he sexually assaulted me in front of my daughter.

I stop this veteran today and helped with some relaxation before continuing.

Female veteran had reported that she tried to address the MST issues on her own and just got more depressed.

The alleged sexual assault occurred probably late in June of, 1991.

/es/Hedi Taylor

MST Counselor

**Signed;** 04/15/2009

---

Authors Note; after the rape, I was numb. I still cannot remember a lot but the one thing that gives me nightmares is during the whole time he was rapping me – I was looking at my daughter. I see her crotched in the corner and her eyes are locked on me.

I am fucking angry!!! Why didn't they pull him off the mission??? Why did this happen? Why did I open the door? Why?Why?Why????

Psychiatrist Note

Unit 8 rounds, female veteran went to classes today; she is comfortable on unit 8 right now "I like it better than the DOM". There was a patient on the unit earlier today that was harassing her, he has left the unit.

"I'm doing better this afternoon" She met with MST counselor today

/es/ Cathy Wilkerson

M.D. Psychiatrist

**Signed;** 04/15/2009

Authors Note; Happy to be safe!

Women's Veteran Support Note

Writer saw patient for a 75 min psychotherapy session for PTSD secondary to MST.

Patient was 5 min late to scheduled session due to forgetting Diary Cards. Diary Cards were reviewed and patient is able to articulate thoughts and feelings in appropriate manner. Early in session, patient becomes angry and starts to cry. Writer had patient stop talking and begins practicing relaxation techniques to center patient. Patient continues therapy session.

Writer discussed Dialectical Behavior Therapy (DBT) skills providing education on therapy and answering all questions patient had. Patient agreed to the following:

GOALS for therapy:

1) Decreasing Suicidal, Para suicidal, and life threatening Behaviors

2) Decreasing or eliminating behaviors that threaten the process of therapy (patient is able to identify possible therapy interfering behaviors)

3) Identify problems that make it possible to develop a reasonable quality of life

RULES for therapy:

1) If patient misses 4 sessions in a row, patient is out of therapy for additional 2 sessions

2) Patient must continue with ongoing individual therapy (patient is not sure who she will be seeing)

3) Patient cannot come to sessions under the influence of alcohol

4) If patient calls someone for help, if patient is feeling suicidal, patient must be willing to accept help

5) If patient is going to miss or be late to a session, patient must call prior to session

6) Patient must complete homework assignment including Diary Cards and bring to session

Next scheduled apt with this writer: April 20

Writer appreciates the opportunity to assist this veteran

/es/ Hedi Taylor

MSW

**Signed;** 04/16/2009

Authors Notes; I really feel like this social worker will help me, she made a plan, she has indicated to me what is to be expected and what we will be doing I am so happy someone has heard my cries for help.

Psychiatrist Note

Unit 8 rounds, met with female veteran 20min, 'I have been happy for the most part'. Working DBT likes the work they are doing. Has a question about discharge. Her husband can pick her up tomorrow after the 1300 class.

We talked about her completing the PCOD program and continuing to work with her MST and DBT counselors. She was also offered a bed on unit 6 if driving back and forth if the driving becomes too much for her.

/es/ Cathy Wilkerson

M.D. psychiatrist

**Signed;** 04/16/2009

Authors Notes; Someone with MST should not have gone to the PCOD program, instead should go to an MST therapy program. I deserve better and so does every female veteran!!!

Social Work Discharge Note

Vet will discharge Unit 8 to her home in Clearmont, WY via POV. Vet's husband will provide transportation. Veteran will attend MHR classes daily and continue to be seen by Dr. Wilkerson

Safety plan was completed w/vet and vet was provided a copy of the plan.

/es/ Loree Bordouex

MSW,

**Signed;** 04/17/2009

Authors Note; so happy to be going home every day, I am so glad the doctor sees this as beneficial for me.

Mental Health Group Note

Female Veteran comes to support group as ongoing treatment

13: number of patients in attendance

PTSD Seeking Safety Group

We reviewed information about self-help groups as well as "substance Abuse and PTSD: Common Questions" Participants commented on their experience with self-help groups and common questions were reviewed.

Behavior of patient:

Active participant:

/es/ Sam Mallory PH.D.

**Signed;** 04/16/2009

Authors Notes; should have had this group lesson when I first came to this program-just saying…..

Mental Health Group Note

Female Veteran comes to support group as ongoing treatment

13 number of patients in attendance

50: minutes spent with patients

We covered the "asking for help" section. Group members commented on the "main points" and discussed how each of these applied to them. The practice assignment for the weekend was to complete the "approach sheet" designed to help them practice asking for help. The next module, "Red and Green Flags" on page 193 was assigned to include completing the "safety plan" on page 195.

Behavior of pt:

Active participant, Made useful disclosures

/es/ Sam Mallory PH.D.

**Signed; 04/17/2009**

Mental Health Group Note

Female Veteran comes to support group as ongoing treatment

12: number of patients in attendance

50: minutes spent with patients.

We reviewed the "asking for help approach sheet" today. We also reviewed "red and green flags". Group members commented on their respective "red and green flags" and made disclosures about same. For next session, group members are to complete the "Create a safety plan" exercise and review the next section which is "Resist: Recovery from substance Use Intensive Skills Training".

Behavior of Patient:

Active participant

/es/ Sam Mallory PH.D.

**Signed; 04/20/2009**

Authors Notes; when is therapy over? Ugh enough! I'm hearing that Amy Winehouse song again no. no. no….. won't go to therapy….

Women's Veteran Support Note

Writer saw patient today for 90 min. DBT psychotherapy session for PTSD. Female Veteran was 10 min early to scheduled session.

Writer began session with practice of mindfulness/breathing exercise. Patient participated and discussed how difficult it was to stay mindful in completing the exercise. Writer began the education on mindfulness and explains we would begin with this DBT module. Patient expressed understanding with the following:

Mindfulness is:

Being in the moment

Awareness

Present mind

A skill as opposed to automatic function

Patient asked several questions and writer acknowledged mindfulness is not meditation, relaxation, spiritual or religious, calming or a means of being emotional. But a way to be able to focus on what is happening 'right now' and not run away. Patient states she understands.

Reasonable, emotional and wise mind were discussed today. Patient asked appropriate questions and was able to provide examples of being in each mindful experience. Patient questioned herself and cried as she discussed her mother and her family. Although patient cried, she was able to bring herself back to present moment. Writer validated patient's ability to reason in her wise mind.

Patient is given homework assignment to continue with Diary Cards and to work on the what? and How of mindfulness. Patient agrees to be mindful of morning ritual and evening ritual without judgment and to document accordingly.

Patient is alert and oriented and able to communicate effectively with this writer. Patient maintains good eye contact, although she wears 2 pairs of glasses to see paperwork presented. Patient cries intermittently when she talks of feeling ashamed. Patient is casually dressed/appropriately groomed. Patient denies any suicidal or homicidal thoughts. It is writer's clinical judgment patient is at low risk to harm self or others at this writing.

/es/ Hedi TaylorMSW

**Signed;** April 20, 2009

Authors Note; I think this is the first time anyone has actually worked with me on what MST problems are and is really trying to get me back to a functioning mood, I really like this therapist.

Psychology Note

Meet with Female veteran for 10 min

Asked veteran today whether she would be interested in engaging in the CHAPS (equine assisted therapy) program? She declines, stating that she has had negative experiences with some of the staff that would be part of the program.

/es/ Sam Mallory, Ph.D.

**Signed;** 4/27/2009

Authors Notes; no, I am not going to this activity! The last activity I went to the VA workers in activities got mad over how many people showed up, so they can kiss my fat ass!

Mental Health group note

10: number of patients in attendance

45: minutes spent with patients

Focus of this group was on getting people to support their recovery; Veterans were given the definitions of supportive, neutral and destructive people regarding their recovery. An example letter of "helpful" information designed to be given to family and friends was read aloud, and discussion followed regarding the efficacy of this letter.

Patient's Goals:

To be aware of who would be supportive and /or destructive in her recovery and an example of information that could be given to family or friends to assist veteran in her recovery.

Progress made:

Uncertain, but it appeared obvious; this veteran was not getting much benefit from this group discussion.

Behavior of patient:

Veteran was difficult to keep on task. She kept inserting her specific issues into the group discussion. When facilitator would redirect to how the seeking safety material would be beneficial in assisting her to set boundaries, she would verbalize disagreement in that it wouldn't work for her. Eventually, this female veteran stated "they threw me in here, where I don't belong, I'm not getting the help I need." I corrected her, stating she was in a treatment group, not a therapy group, and I tried to explain why it was not conducive to discuss specific trauma issues in a group setting, and none of the current groups at this VA were geared to that aspect. She then put her hand up, as if to say "enough" and proceeded to get up and walk out of class.

/es/ Claud Cline

MSW

**Signed;** 04/29/2009

Authors Note; I don't like Chlamydia! She irritates me! This isn't the place for me; I need MST help not combat PTSD help. Why was I referred to this program? I'll never understand.

Psychiatrist Note

Female Veteran came to my door "I'm having a meltdown". Her MST therapist was available and came in and we helped her work through it. She does see that she has been making progress. She is able to talk with her husband as well and this is helpful. She did not think that it would be as difficult as it has been, she keeps wanting to be "better' and that she can have a normal life" without the entire struggle. Sometimes she would like to quit "and not be here anymore... I'm tired, I don't want to deal with people's crap, I don't want to deal with my Dad dying... and then I have to come here", she realizes she has to "focus" on the solution and to make progress no matter how slight. I'm working on it, getting better, just a meltdown in chlamydia's group. Once again must correct veteran from calling names and to refer to her as Claudia not an STD.

42 year white female with chronic PTSD/MST, depression, anxiety, difficulty with somatic issues, Female Veteran has made some progress. The DAV hearing was re-scheduled and she will have to go again after the program is completed and she is rehearsing a catastrophic outcome around it. Her MST therapist helped her with re-routing herself expectations, she responded well and was able to self soothe effectively using her new coping tools.

/es/ Cathy Wilkerson

M.D. Psychiatrist

**Signed;** Apr/29/2009

Authors Notes; I don't like chlamydia, and yes she's like an STD cause she irritates me.

My father is dying of colon cancer and I feel terrible that I can't help with his care.

Women's Veteran Support Note

Writer saw female veteran for 90 min

Patient engaged in learning mindfulness 'how' skills in DBT. Patient was able to articulate and give examples of being non-judgmental, being one mindfully, and being effective in the show of mindfulness. Patient reports she completed her exercises the previous week in regards to mindfulness practice and found it difficult to stay mindful. Writer acknowledged the difficulty to stay mindful. Writer acknowledged the difficulty and explained why it is important of radical acceptance even when the patient felt otherwise. Writer and patient went over some examples and patient states 'I understand'. Patient will practice being mindful and taking a non-evaluative approach over the next week.

Patient also reports she has been going to sleep about 5pm and has been sleeping until 5am. Writer screened for reasoning and patient reports 'I don't know'. I am tired." Writer encourage patient to stay up and become active instead of giving in to her tiredness. Writer reiterated radical acceptance and how she can use radical acceptance instead of giving into the tiredness or depression. Patient denies any depression. Patient agrees to try to stay awake and will attempt to engage family in her current thoughts and feelings.

Writer discussed patient's behavior in the classroom over the last week. Patient admits it did not help anyone or change any situation by her getting up and leaving. Again, writer and patient discussed and applied radical acceptance to the situation. Patient agrees to stay in classes for the remainder of her time in therapy.

Patient is alert and oriented and able to communicate with this writer. Patient is dressed/groomed appropriately; maintains excellent eye contact throughout session; and no abnormal movements are noted. Patient denied any suicidal thoughts or homicidal thoughts. Because of past attempts and because of patient declaration of depressive actions, it is writer's clinical judgment patient is at low to moderate risk to harm self. Writer and patient talked about actions patient could take if she should feel like harming self. Patient agrees to contact her husband.

Female Veteran is to continue with therapy groups and to continue seeing this writer for DBT Skills Training. Patient agrees to stop by the MST therapist office today to make a follow up appointment.

Writer appreciates the opportunity to assist this veteran

/es/ Hedi Taylor

MSW

**Signed;** April 30, 2009

Authors Note; finally! Cannot say it enough how much I like this social worker. She is helping me by apply techniques that work with MST issues. Listen up therapist techniques that work!!!! Not fucking drugs!!!!

Psychiatrist Note

Discharge, PCOD program strengths—" the PTSD class helped me the most", "after the first four weeks was able to talk to counselors one on one"; weaknesses—not enough staff to help veterans with needs, women need an MST program here, women's groups, get women their own section to live.

Re. PTSD. She had a difficult course while she was here, she says 'it was worse than hard" and she was triggered continually when she was living on campus, i.e. seeing certain doorways in the building reminded her of the room where she was raped, there was another patient living in the building who looked like the man who raped her, etc. She ended up getting over activated one day and cutting her arms superficially to try to lower her level of distress. This resulted in a few days on the locked psychiatric unit where she stabilized. After discharge she was allowed to attend classes from home, where she stabilized. After discharge she was allowed to attend classes from home, where she was more stable and comfortable. She has grown in her ability to cope but is nowhere near working through the issues from her MST/PTSD; she needs ongoing weekly contacts for therapy. Staff tried to be there for her but she felt that there was not enough supportive structure here, especially in the early weeks. She met with her case manager and others to express her concerns and tried to take a solution oriented approach to getting her needs met, however, this was still not enough to prevent her from getting flooded. She eventually learned how to deal with her emotions and made great deal of progress along this line. This female veteran will continue with outpatient therapy.

Re: mood. At the beginning her depression and anxiety were fairly severe. With treatment and medications she has stabilized. She struggled a great deal in this process and by discharge her more mature personality is becoming evident more and more. However, her PTSD symptoms from the MST/PTSD are a continual factor in trying to destabilize her.

Re. relationships, she got along with some peers but not others. She had a tendency to be resistive with some staff and it was difficult for her to see her part. She is aware that she needs to make some amends as she moves forward, to deal with her part and not to worry about others. We discussed her continuing to work on this but from a perspective where she will not put herself down further in the process, rather, from a perspective where she will be able to understand what she is doing while maintaining the perspective that she is doing the right thing and feeling good about it vs. feeling more defective/defensive.

Re. medical issues, she felt she had health problems but workups continue to be negative. Her neurologist saw her and there were some concerns.

Re. disposition, returning home, continuing to work with the women's health program director on DBT, continuing to work with the MST counselor.

42 year white female with chronic PTSD/MST, depression, anxiety, difficulty with somatic issues. Stable at discharge. Will follow up with MST therapist and DBT therapist after discharge.

Plan: --discharge as plan

/es/ Cathy Wilkerson

M.D. Psychiatrist

**Signed;** 05/05/2009

Authors Note; Yesssssss!!!!!! Done with therapy one more class and this bitch is outta here..........

Mental Health Group Note

12: number of patients

50 minutes spent with patient

Progress made: NONE

Behavior of patient: This female veteran informed me when walked into the class room that she was graduating today, and was to get certificate, and she was done today. I tried to explain to her that I knew nothing about it, and her discharge date is 5/7/2009. She informed me I was wrong, and she didn't care what the sheet said; she was leaving today and she better get her certificate. I again tried to explain that I knew nothing about it. She stated that Dr. Wilkerson had told her she would give her a discharge apt for this date, and Dr. Wilkerson said she could be done today. At that point I asked her to leave the classroom, as she was being disruptive to others in the class. She informed me I could call the VA police because she was not leaving without her certificate. I then went to Dr. Wilkerson's office and requested she come and get this veteran as she was being disruptive to the class and would not leave. Dr. Wilkerson then came into the hall, and once this veteran saw her coming toward the classroom, she got up and pointed at me and stated, I'm right, you're wrong" and then walked out of the classroom. This veteran was very disruptive to the class and other veteran's voiced that they were upset by her actions.

/es/Claud Cline

MSW

**Signed**; 05/05/2009

Author's Note; damn straight I didn't learn shit from this therapy cause IT WAS THE WRONG PLACE FOR ME!! I can't stand this bitch all she had to do was go and ask the Dr. If I was to graduate or better yet just believe that I am telling the truth but, nooooo instead Chlamydia had to make this little power play in front of the others and I wasn't going to back down! Fucking STD Bitch!!

I did leave the program and I got my certificate of completion. I just had to wait until the afternoon class to get it – yup! humility sucking it up right now.

## Chapter

# 13

Author's Note; I wish to thank the VA hospital for all the hard work they do to support and maintain the care for our veterans. The VA is working hard at making sure every VA has a woman's health coordinator for there are more and more females entering and serving in the armed forces than ever before. The VA finally put in a women's health coordinator in the Sheridan VA, that simple act saved my life. Thankyou VA for starting to think of us female veterans and stepping away from the same old VA system of our grandfathers.

The following mental health notes are from the 1st Women's Health Coordinator established at the Sheridan Wyoming Veterans Hospital. There were a few notes in previous chapters, but the following notes are from the one on one which has greatly helped me become the person I am today. I would like other therapist at other Veteran Hospitals around the country to take notice of how she finished her notes with; this writer appreciates working with this veteran. That one sentence means she cared and I wasn't just a number.

I would like to also note that this social worker started the first women's co-hort in Sheridan, Wyoming. A Co-Hort is for women only, and helps female veterans cope with what women go thru like combat and rape.

## Women's Veteran Support Note May 12, 2009

Writer saw Female Veteran for 90 min today

Patient presented with DBT homework completed. Patient showed slight improvement in being able to practice Mindfulness; however, Patient and writer discussed previous week issues concerning program discharge. Patient admits she became angry and was asked to leave the class. Writer and Patient continued to discuss what skills patient could have used to alter the outcome of the event. Patient acknowledges "I guess I could have agreed to disagree and moved forward until after class ended but, I don't like Chlamydia. Writer acknowledges her frustration with mental health worker and asked patient to refrain from calling her names.

Writer continued to work on mindfulness and providing handouts and requested the patient to continue in her practice daily, Several times a day. Patient agrees to do so.

Patient is alert and oriented and able to communicate with this writer effectively. Patient is dressed/groomed appropriately; patient maintains good eye contact and no abnormal movements are noted. Patient denies harm to self and others.

Writer appreciates the opportunity to assist this veteran.

/es/ Hedi Taylor

MSW

Authors Note; Being mindful is difficult but with daily practice I have been able to maintain a conversation with out my mind wondering or switching from subject to subject.

## Women's Veteran's Support Note June 15, 2009

Writer met with Female Veteran for 90 min today.

Patient and writer began by writer providing introduction to distress tolerance and patient is able to provide examples and discuss what she should have done in deflecting the crisis instead of getting angry. Writer continued to advise patient of the skills she will learn over the next 4-5 weeks including but not limited to: distraction, self – soothing techniques, improving in the moment, and thinking of pros and cons of a situation. Writer and patient discussed PTSD symptoms and the avoidance of such symptoms causing additional pain and suffering. As we discussed the patients sexual trauma patient begins to cry. Patient acknowledged avoidance of all painful experiences because she was so angry. Writer encourage patient to think of her thoughts and the underlying feelings of anger. Writer continued education/skills class by expressing the acceptance of reality is not equivalent to approval of reality. Patient expressed understanding.

Writer appreciates the opportunity to assist this veteran.

/es/ Hedi TaylorMSW

Authors Note; I am still angry with how the Army dealt with the mission I was on. I am however trying to move forward with my future and the possibilities that life has for me. I have an idea that I want to patent and see what the world of invention can do for me and my family who knows what can happen- I am such a dreamer. haha

## Women's Health Support Note July 8, 2009

Writer met with female veteran for 90 min today

Patient is alert and oriented and able to communicate appropriately with this writer. Patient reports mood as "I 'am doing much better'; affect is appropriate to mood and content. Patient is dressed well groomed appropriately. Patient maintains good thoughts no plan of self-harm or harm to others. It is writer's clinical judgment patient is at low risk to harm self or others at this time.

Writer appreciates the opportunity to assist this veteran.

/es/ Hedi Taylor

MSW

Authors Note; I do feel better. Mentally - no, cause the nightmares haven't gone away and the anxiety is still high and let's not forget that my left hand is a constant reminder of the rape –it will never stop shaking.

## Women's Health Support Note July 14, 2009

Writer saw female veteran for 75 min.

Writer provides 2nd session of distress tolerance skills of DBT. Patient is able to articulate understanding of being critical and judgmental over issues and how this often skews patient view of issues often making her angry. Patient identified a recent issue that occurred at church and how she dealt with the issue by using Mindfulness Skills. Writer validated patient ability to use the skills and encouraged continued use.

Writer and patient discussed patients recent missed appointments and writer addressed DBT contract signed by pt. Patient agrees to stay with DBT and comply with contract. Patient completes homework from before.

Prior to leaving patient reports 'I feel better; I think this is the only place I can be heard". Writer provided support and encouraged patient to talk with her husband about her thoughts and feelings. Patient agrees to think about it.

Writer appreciates the opportunity to assist this veteran.

/es/ Hedi Taylor

MSW

Oops I did miss some appointments I should write an excuse right now but like my dad always said "excuses are like assholes everyone has one"

Women's Health Support Note August 13, 2009

Writer met with female veteran for 45min.

Patient reports that she's discourage over recent weight gain. Writer assisted patient with setting realistic goals concerning her weight loss and encouraged her with starting a plan. Writer provided limited education on fibromyalgia, depression, anxiety and eating habits and how food intake can hinder mental health issues. Patient acknowledged understanding.

Patient states she is feeling better overall this week and reports she has been using her DBT skills of mindfulness and staying in the moment. Writer validates patient's willingness to recognize the need and also encouraged patient on skills of radical acceptance. Writer also attempted to help patient with the current psychiatrist note on physiological issues. Patient expressed understanding. Patient talked about wanting to return to work part time but is concerned about her health and being off of work for so long. Writer and patient talked about Voc Rehab and the possibility of working part-time at the Sheridan VAMC to reintegrate back into the work force.

Writer appreciates the opportunity to assist this veteran.

/es/ Hedi Taylor

MSW

Authors Notes; I have gained some weight – I have concluded that if I get my benefits from the VA then I will have that weight lose surgery in hopes of being healthier and maybe my self-esteem will grow instead of my pant size. Haha

Women's Support Health Note

Writer received phone call from veteran requesting appointment. Writer advised appointment had been made and provided date of appointment. Writer apologized for not getting back with patient over the last couple of days and advised of long distance problem. Veteran expressed understanding. Veteran reports she is doing well and has been busy with canning. Veteran also reports she has not been hurting as much since she started taking medication for seizures. Writer provided support and validated veteran staying busy.

Veteran denies any current thoughts of harm. Vet sounds good and up beat during phone call.

Writer appreciates the opportunity to assist this veteran.

Apt: Oct 2 @ 10

## Women's Support Health Note October 02, 2009

Writer met with Female Veteran for 30min.

Patient reports she is doing "well "today and overall mood from last week has been "fine". Patient does report feeling tired and aches all over. Writer provided support as needed.

Writer assisted patient in challenging any maladaptive thoughts she would have concerning this subject and assisted patient in radical acceptance. Patient states "I' am trying".

Patient continues to report her relationship with husband is good; however. She feels he is always trying to fix things. Writer and patient discussed further and writer provided education on mental health diagnosis and family involvement. Writer offered to speak to patient with her husband. Patient will think about it.

Writer advised patient she would be out of town next week and if there were an emergency to please contact the emergency help line.

Writer appreciates the opportunity to assist this veteran.

/es/ Hedi Taylor

MSW

Authors Notes; my husband is constantly worried about how I'm feeling? Do I need anything? Ugh, leave me alone I'm fine now, I just need to be left alone.

## Women's Support Health Note December 03, 2009

Writer met with female veteran for 55 min today.

Patient is on time for scheduled session

For the first half of session patient discussed her father's illness and reports the doctors told the family this week that her dad probably only has a couple of weeks to live. Writer remained quiet and let patient continue with her thoughts. Writer remained quiet and let patient continue with her thoughts. Patient is able to identify special moments with her father and discussed saying goodbye.

Patient talked about not being able to sleep well at night but finds she is tired all the time. Writer provided education on anticipatory grief and advised patient to nap as she needed but also not to stay in bed all the time. Patient reports she gets up daily and dresses but sometimes it is difficult.

Patient is alert and oriented and able to express thoughts and feelings appropriately. It is writer's clinical judgment patient is at low risk to harm self or others at this writing.

Writer appreciates the opportunity to assist this veteran.

/es/ Hedi Taylor

MSW

Authors Notes; my father was a good man and I often referred him to John Wayne character's. He wasn't always right and he wasn't always wrong but when he talked to me he had a since of wisdom behind the words. I Loved Him!

## Women's Support Health Note February 08, 2009

Writer met with female veteran for 50 min today

Patient reports "I'm doing ok" You know I hate coming up here, I really do. Writer screened patient for understanding and patient begins to report on issues she feels are unfair concerning past treatment procedures. Patient also remarks it is difficult because "I'm always reminded of what happened to me while I was in the military'. Writer validates patient's ability to acknowledge her disappointments and challenged patient's maladaptive thoughts concerning previous treatment.

Patient continues to discuss her family and her father's recent death. Patient begins to cry as she discusses her dad. Writer remained quiet and provided support as needed.

Patient discussed future treatments and request to be seen every other month if possible. Patient also discussed her trauma and cries as she does so. Writer encouraged patient to think about Prolong Exposure Treatment but patient reports 'I don't like it up here and I don't want to talk about the rape! If I do not think about it maybe it will go away'. Writer provides some education on rational for trauma therapy and PTSD reactions including avoidance. Patient acknowledged she understands she avoids and wants to keep it this way.

Writer appreciates the opportunity to assist this veteran.

/es/ Hedi Taylor MSW

Authors Note; I really miss my father, death of a loved one is never easy and There is no time line for grief, I don't care what people say about that, I will always miss my father.

I do not like coming to the VA because it does remind me of the Army and this causes me panic and sometimes I wish the therapist would understand how hard it is for some veterans to come up there.

## Women's Support Health Note April 28, 2009

Writer met with female veteran for 55min.

During the last 30 min of patient visit writer advised patient this writer would be leaving the Sheridan VAMC. Patient attempted to console this writer and to encourage writer. Writer asked patient about feelings and then patient cries. Patient has concerns over new therapist and writer validates patient thoughts and feelings.

Patient begins to cry and thanks writer for all she has done to help her over the last year. Writer reminded patient that she had done all the work and this writer was only the catalyst to assist the patient with mental health.

Patient ended session by asking for a hug from this writer. Of Note, throughout the last year session's patient has always talked about how difficult it was for her to hug people including her family. Writer validates patient again for how far she has come and patient leaves by Thanking the writer.

It has indeed been a pleasure to assist this veteran.

/es/ Hedi TaylorMSW

Authors Note; Hedi Taylor was the best therapist I ever had!! She worked with me not against me, she didn't push pills but what she did push was self-acceptance and self-awareness. Hedi also taught me to be me again, to laugh and to step out of the deep end of depression. I am not a second class soldier! I am a soldier who did her job and got raped.

I received an Army Achievement Medal for that secret mission I went on but it's been 20 years and I still haven't received it, but one day it will come in the mail and I'll pin to my shirt and wear it for a week, then I'll put it in my purse and show people for about a week and then I'll put it on a shelf and every now and then I'll look at it and say "Damn girl, you did something great once and you should be proud"

One more thing…… this writer appreciates Hedi Taylor!

The Female Veteran

I am not a disabled veteran
I am a decorated veteran

I am not courageous
I am fearless

I am not a victim
I am a warrior

I am not just a soldier
I am a woman

By Ty Will

www.ingramcontent.com/pod-product-compliance
Lightning Source LLC
LaVergne TN
LVHW011724060526
838200LV00051B/3012